Praise

"Yet another example of the incredible resiliency of the human spirit. A testament to the strength we can all access inside ourselves when faced with extreme adversity. It begs the question what would you do…"
– Rebecca Bailey, PhD, author of *Safe Kids, Smart Parents*

"Jessica triumphs over tragedy and brings joy to the lives of everyone around her and everyone who will read this book. The dichotomy of what it is like to love an abusive parent is rarely talked about and she does so in a beautifully profound way. This book speaks to the importance of holding abusers accountable but also forgiveness for our own hearts. She paves the way for individuals who have experienced trauma to break the cycle of abuse by being incredibly honest and vulnerable about her own experiences, struggles and perseverance."
– Savannah J. Sanders, survivor and author of *Sex Trafficking Prevention: A Trauma-Informed Approach for Parents and Professionals*

"Jessica overcame obstacles most of us cannot fathom. She continues to be a beacon of hope and light to women and children by offering them a chance to succeed. As a child advocate I applaud her efforts!"
– Pam Gaber, CEO and Founder of Gabriel's Angels (pet therapy for at-risk children) and author of *Gabriel's Angels–The Story of the Dog Who Inspired a Revolution*

"Jessica brings a passion and energy in her support for organizations that address child abuse and domestic violence that is contagious. She does so from personal experience and a sincere desire to protect others from abuse and violence. As a police chief, it is encouraging to have Jessica working alongside of law enforcement for the safety of others."
– Jerald L. Monahan, Prescott, Arizona Police Chief, past Chairperson of the Arizona Governor's Commission to Prevent Violence Against Women

Baba's Daughter

Memoirs of a Persian-American Girl

Jessica Shahriari Nicely

UNHOOKED BOOKS
an imprint of High Conflict Institute Press
Scottsdale, Arizona

Publisher's Note
This publication is designed to provide accurate and authoritative information about the subject matter covered. It is sold with the understanding that neither the author nor publisher are rendering legal, mental health, medical, or other professional services, either directly or indirectly. If expert assistance, legal or psychological services is needed, the services of a competent professional should be sought. Neither the author nor the publisher shall be liable or responsible for any loss or damage allegedly arising as a consequence of your use or application of any information or suggestions in this book.

Author's Note
This is a work of nonfiction. Some names and identifying details have been altered in order to protect particular individuals. Everything herein is based on the author's own memories and recollections.

Library of Congress Control Number: 2014952321

We thank and acknowledge the following for the permission to reprint excerpts from the following previously published material:
  Dust Tracks on a Road by Zora Neale Hurston, Harper Perennial
  The Hiding Place by Corrie Ten Boom, Baker Publishing Group

Cover design by Gordan Blazevik
Interior design by Jeff Fuller, Shelfish.weebly.com
Edited by Wylie O'Sullivan
Cover photograph by Martin Christopher

Printed in the United States of America

For all the other survivors who
wished their childhoods away.

"I have been in Sorrow's kitchen and licked out all the pots. Then I have stood on the peaky mountain wrapped in rainbows, with a harp and sword in my hands."

– Zora Neale Hurston

Contents

Introduction: Scattered Fragments

My plan was to do as literally hundreds of people have told me I should over the years: write down the story of my apparently fascinating life. The story that has made counselors cry and sit baffled that I am a functioning member of society, the story that helped earn me a spot on the stage at the Miss USA pageant, the story that helped me become the woman I am today. But when I actually sat down to do it, I realized that my memories are so fractured and small that I can only write it the way I recall it all—in scattered fragments. I don't know if the gaps in my memory are typical or if they're because of the trauma I experienced during childhood. There have probably been thousands of studies done about how the brain forgets certain things, and sometimes entire periods of time, to protect itself. Maybe my brain is trying to protect me from my own experiences. If so, I don't think that protection actually serves its purpose anymore: I want to remember what happened to me so I can make peace with it and move forward in my own life. I want to write it down because I hope my story of suffering abuse as a child and emerging into a happy, productive adulthood might help other people. And so here they are, the fragments of my life.

Luckily, I've always been a writer; I write down pretty much everything. I also enjoy the blessing of being a bit of a hoarder—I don't throw anything away. So much of what is in this book is from the poems, journals, and calendars I've kept all these years.

I'm sure some people will be upset by what they read, and some might even get angry with me for sharing parts of my history that involve them. What I describe may not be exactly the way they remember it, but isn't that always the case? Two people can see or experience the exact same thing and then describe it later in two completely different fashions. I've tried to be as honest as possible with my memories, and as fair as possible, while still telling the story—*my* story.

Do you ever catch a whiff of someone's perfume or smell a food that triggers a memory of a time in your life? Certain moments from my childhood come rushing back every time I encounter particular sensory triggers. Sometimes I'll see something, sometimes it's a smell, and just like that I'm back in my childhood, scared and lonely. One such trigger is a cookie I used to love that I haven't eaten in over thirty years because of an especially bad day when we were living in my grandmother's house.

I had come into the kitchen to get a grasshopper cookie, which is similar to an Oreo but with a minty cream filling; I loved them. I remember walking down the hall from my room into the kitchen, seeing Daddy, and knowing immediately that he was mad—and, as was almost always the case, I had no idea why. I hesitated, looking at him, and he turned and glared back at me and shouted, "WHAT? What are you doing in here? What do you want?"

"I was going to get a cookie," I said in the most non-confrontational voice I could muster. I knew his tone; I had heard it many times before. It meant I was about to be in trouble for no good reason. Before I could think another thought, I was dodging a bag of rice that he'd hurled at my head, then the package of grasshopper cookies, a loaf of bread, a can of soup, a bag of chickpeas, and a jar of peanut butter. He opened the fridge. "Do you want milk too?" The milk flew across the room. I was standing in a pile of food; the mess was all over the kitchen by now. It went on until my grandmother came in and made him knock it off. He stormed off, shoving into me on his way out, glaring at me like I'd just killed his new puppy.

That moment in the kitchen—him throwing things at me, my confusion about why he was so angry, that feeling of helplessness, knowing I had to stand there and take it or he'd just get angrier, because in that moment of fury Daddy had to do that to me—that feeling dominated my childhood. Nothing made sense, rage was thrown around for no reason, anger loomed everywhere you looked. I was in a constant state of anxiety over when this rage would strike next, because there generally was no precursor; it just attacked you out of nowhere.

— — —

Herbert Ward, a veteran in the world of child abuse prevention, once said, "Child abuse casts a shadow the length of a lifetime." There is so much truth in that—the shadow has always followed me around, presenting itself in lots of different ways throughout my life. Even in some of my most joyful moments, the harrowing memories still loom. The abuse left me a wounded person, and still, after all these years, I am embarrassed to admit it. In some ways, it's also made me tougher and stronger: I don't get bent out of shape about nonsense; I definitely have a fighter's instinct; and, I have to say, I could probably win in most situations. But even though it's painful to expose myself, I want other survivors, as well as children and women being abused right now, to know that I am not saying I walked away completely unscathed.

The biggest damage resulted not from the punches or the slaps, but from the emotional abuse. Thanks to that, I still struggle sometimes with trusting people, even the ones who love me. Occasionally, on bad days, I am fully confident that everyone who loves me will leave, damaging my heart on their way out the door. For years I needed constant love and attention, and when I didn't get it, I truly felt less than normal—and again, I still have my moments. "Hellos" and "good-byes" are very important to me, and I'm very sensitive to tone of voice. When I'm feeling shaky and someone says they love me, I need to hear it in their voice.

But these things are getting easier for me. I used to fake happiness and confidence and poise. Today, when I seem contented or calm or comfortable, I usually actually feel that way inside, at least partly. I believe that the important people in my life truly do love me. I know that what I have to say is worthwhile and that I'm allowed to want things for myself.

What all of this adds up to—and what I've been told more than once—is that I'm a dichotomy. I'm a super-sensitive girl who can't watch anything scary before I go to sleep; I have to watch and look at happy images so that I don't have nightmares. And yet I love to watch mixed martial arts fighting, the bloodier the better. I'm a pageant girl who hates to fix her hair, hates to shop for clothes and shoes. While I have an extreme and often irrational fear of being abandoned, I do not fear being alone. In fact, I quite enjoy being by myself, when I'm feeling good. My feelings can be as fragile as an eggshell some days, while other times I can get my heart broken and laugh it off. It all depends on the moment.

Because I was raised in chaos, fear, and sadness, I am essentially two people: I am sometimes braver than brave, ready to take on anyone or anything at any moment—especially any man ready to hit a woman or child—which I do fairly often. And then other times I'm still that quiet, invisible little girl, scared and sad and lonely even when surrounded by people.

I can imagine the conclusions and diagnoses counselors and therapists might make about me—I've read about all the personality disorders. And while I may have glimmers of some of them, in balance, that is not who I am. Yes, I am damaged in spots, and I make plenty of mistakes. And yes, some days I feel so lonely I ache. But overall I really feel pretty normal most of the time.

— — —

This book is about how I not only survived all of that, but have found a happiness and peace I never imagined was possible for me. The journey has involved many blessings, mixed in with the pain. Throughout my life, I was lucky enough to encounter a lot of good people, starting with many of my childhood friends and their families, who welcomed me into their calm, happy homes. I also had some wonderful schoolteachers who took me under their wings, and I always nurtured a belief that I could grow up and be like them. Those people were lights in my life who showed me that there was hope for something more, something better. Truly, it's thanks to them that I've been able to cobble together the fragments of my life and memory, and my dichotomized personality, into a whole person.

I've also always taken great solace and comfort from nature. As a kid, I always spent as much time outside, away from our miserable home, as possible. We lived in a very pretty, woodsy town full of flowers and trees, and I think it helped keep me sane.

Maybe the most significant thing that allowed me to heal was forgiving my father. It wasn't easy, and it took a long time. But in the end, trying to understand his life, his experience, and what drove him toward abusive behavior, and then finding the strength to forgive him for it, has saved me as much as anything else.

Feeling like a complete person is an ongoing project, of course. It still takes a lot of self-awareness and effort, and some days are better than others. But for the most part, I revel in the rich, full life I've created. What follows is the whole story of how I got here.

CHAPTER 1

Daddy isn't here to read this story today. He can't give his account, or counter all the negative with all that he did right. And so I will do it for him. Number one, he stuck around when my "mom" didn't and he stayed long enough to teach my sister and me a lot of good qualities. He often told me he loved me— "I love you, Jes-SEE-ka," that's how he said my name. He made sure we always lived in a safe, beautiful home, in a safe, beautiful neighborhood. We were never once hungry and we were always clean and well dressed. Daddy ensured that my sister and I got college educations. He taught us to be empathetic and giving. He taught us to always use good manners. He passed along an immense love for animals—we always had pets, usually cats. Our first cat, gray and fluffy and sweet, was named Mouse. I have had cats pretty much ever since. Daddy taught us to be strong in the face of adversity, even when that adversity came at his hand. He did a lot of things wrong, but Daddy also did a lot for my sister and me, and for what he gave us, both the good and the bad, I will be forever grateful.

It took me a long time to forgive my father, but for the most part, I have. And while that has been one of the most difficult things I've done, it's also, really, been the most important, because it's allowed me to move past my terrible childhood and forward into my life today. I suppose a big part of forgiveness is understanding: If we can understand where someone comes from—the hardships they've endured, the pain they carry— then we can imagine why they might have gone on to inflict pain on other people. It's so often cyclical. That doesn't make it okay by any means. But it makes it possible to comprehend, which is the beginning of forgiveness. So I'll go back even further than my childhood and tell you some of Daddy's story, which began in Tehran, the capital of Iran.

— — —

When you think of the Middle East, you probably think of camels and deserts. It's partially true in Daddy's case—his family really did have a camel when he was growing up—but there is a lot more greenery in the Iranian desert than you'd think. I'm told that Tehran, coincidentally, looks an awful lot like Phoenix, Arizona, where I've lived all my adult years.

— — —

Daddy was the first of five children born to a colonel in the Iranian Air Force and my sweet grandmother, Parisa, who stayed home to care for the children. They were quite an affluent, prominent family; in fact, my grandfather was evidently very close with the Shah. I gather that things were pretty good in his family; they were relatively happy and functional. Of course, my grandfather was an Iranian man, who lived by those norms. He occasionally hit his children—I know of one specific incident when my dad lied or stole something—but in Iran he wouldn't have been considered abusive. And the stories I've heard suggest that he was actually quite sensitive. He wrote poetry in his spare time. And my grandmother was one of the most patient people on the planet.

But the family's peace and stability was destroyed when the Shah became suspicious that my grandfather had betrayed him, sometime during my father's childhood. I don't know the details—all I've been told is that the Shah would have had most people jailed—but because of their close relationship, instead he had my grandfather demoted so that he no longer had any power in the air force. My grandfather was devastated, and the stress of it caused a stroke and, eventually, his death.

As a young man, my father had wanted to follow in his father's footsteps and become a pilot in the air force. I don't know why, but it did not happen, and I think it was a crushing blow for him. In early 1968 or late 1967, unhappy with his own prospects as well as with the Iranian government, Daddy left for the United States, settling in Washington, DC; he was twenty-six or twenty-seven. My grandmother came some years later, when I was about five years old, and various other relatives gradually made their way to the DC area.

Here is where the stripper called "the Snake" enters the story—the Snake, aka Patty, aka my "mom." I put that in quotation marks because I don't really think of her as my mother; she gave birth to me, but that's it. She left when my sister, Serena, and I were very young, and I've had little interaction with her since. She worked in a dirty, smoky, gross club called Dream Dolls, and she and her full C cups were evidently mesmerizing. She didn't discriminate—she'd sidle down beside whoever was sitting near the stage and allow them to slip a few more bills into her lacey thong. Patty had chestnut brown hair all the way down to her waist, hollow brown eyes, and a body like Jessica Rabbit's, all God given. The patrons of Dream Dolls no doubt thanked God for this blessing on a regular basis.

It gets better: Daddy ran the strip club. How's that for a "how we met" story? With his movie-star good looks—he had a bone structure girls would die for, and piercing black eyes—and his role as boss, I'm sure he seemed quite the catch to Patty, at least for a while, enough so that Patty and Daddy married and started a family.

From the outside looking in, Dream Dolls probably seemed like just another little shop on Wisconsin Avenue. But inside its walls were countless lost souls, both on stage and in the audience. The club is sandwiched between two eateries, the kind that seem to change hands on an annual basis; at last check, it was a pizza joint and a sushi place. It's just a block away from some lovely shops and very close to the nation's monuments, but Dream Dolls feels a million miles away from that world of light and order. It's strange to think I exist solely because of this dark, sad, lonely place that is a last resort for young girls who have lost their way and an escape for lonely, horny men. Yuck. What a way to start. But it's my start; it's where the story of me begins.

I often marvel that Daddy ended up in that establishment, that he went from the capital of Iran to the capital of the United States—from beautiful but rule-laden Tehran to this tiny strip club where the men and women seemed free of any type of rules or structure at all. I'm not sure how he got the job; I know the owner of the club was Persian. It was Daddy's first job in the States, and it set the course for his future work life. I imagine it was painful for him, given his dream of becoming a pilot like his father. He absolutely loved airplanes and jets; he was really kind of obsessed with them. Throughout my childhood he had pictures of jets all over our basement walls, and he built model jet planes. He would go to Dulles Airport and just watch the planes fly. Sometimes he would take me and my sister with him.

He never talked about it, but his unfulfilled dream, combined with his shame over working at a strip club, must have contributed to his enormous sense of failure, which he would carry with him his whole life. I'm sure it was humiliating for him to come down in the world, after growing up with a father who once had such an impressive career.

Shortly after I was born, the Snake shed her skin—that is, she left us. I would learn much later her ever-so-predictable reason for leaving: She ran off with a man she met at the strip club. He was a musician and, as the story goes, a very talented and successful one, at least for a time. I was told that she left us to follow José Feliciano, whose big hit, "Feliz Navidad," was played on radio stations around the world every Christmas season throughout my childhood; to my chagrin, it still is. For the record, even though I heard this story from more than one person in my family, on more than one occasion, for years, there's always a chance someone got it wrong—I wanted to say that, just in case it wasn't actually José Feliciano.

Growing up, Christmas in our house was always a little different from everyone else's, though I suppose that could be said of many things involving my family. Most of the Christmases I remember were in our house on Carrleigh Parkway, a very cute street lined with brick townhomes. Some houses had blue front doors, some had black, with shutters to match. We had an end unit, with a huge pine tree in the side yard. Throughout my childhood, our houses were always decorated the same: Persian carpets over the hardwood floors, dark colors, good antique furniture—Daddy only ever wanted "the good kind" of everything. The idea is so burned into my brain that I still use that term to this day. I'm forever saying, "Oh, you have to get the good kind," though I'm usually referring to toilet paper or something trivial like that, not antique furnishings.

In any case our houses were always well kept, uncluttered, comfortable. If you peeked in our living room window on a Christmas morning before everyone awoke, you would have thought a perfectly normal family lived in that charming townhouse. The peaceful and pleasant appearance of our home betrayed none of the turmoil that flared inside it much of the time, including every single Christmas I can remember. I wonder if it was partially his defiant nature and the fact that he knew he was supposed to be extra loving and kind on that day that made Daddy rebel and be exceptionally cantankerous on Christmas.

Every single year for the seventeen years I lived at home,

as we pulled out that same artificial Christmas tree and stuck the color-coordinated branches into its trunk, we always listened to the same Christmas music. We had a box set of four records—the box was a deep red decorated with a picture of an elaborate Christmas ornament—containing songs by Bing Crosby, Nat King Cole, all the traditional Christmas fare. It wasn't until years later that I heard that Patty left us for the famous singer, so I didn't understand why Daddy always forbade the radio at Christmastime. Occasionally, at a friend's house, I'd hear more current Christmas music—Hall and Oats had a song I liked—and so every year I'd ask if we could turn on the radio to hear some different songs. I always got a harsh "No!" for an answer. Daddy was always in an especially terrible mood during the holidays.

One Christmas morning when I was little, I got a doll I had really wanted. I remember she wore a pretty yellow cloth dress and looked very lifelike, except for her huge plastic head and plastic baby hair. I was thrilled when I unwrapped her. I squealed and laughed, which prompted Daddy to berate me for a good twenty minutes about how shallow I was. That wasn't the word he used—his English vocabulary wasn't that extensive—but in essence that's what he said: how super shallow I was for being so happy about a stupid doll and what kind of person was I that I would get so happy about material things. I never played with that doll, and I never again made the mistake of being too happy about anything I received in that house.

When we were very little, before Patty left, my dad's brother Hassan moved from Iran to the United States, and he lived with us for a time. Apparently, Patty and Uncle Hassan did not get along. Daddy and Hassan would hang around, smoking and drinking and speaking Farsi, and Patty felt left out. I guess all cheaters need an excuse for why they cheat, and that may have been hers—she may have been feeling neglected by Daddy because he was paying too much attention to my uncle.

When she left, my sister was two and a half, I was eight months old, and Daddy was overwhelmed. Here he was alone in a foreign country with an imperfect grasp of the language, in a job he despised, and now left by the woman he loved to raise two children by himself. He did have a little help from his brother, who was my favorite uncle. But it wasn't enough—Daddy must have been truly miserable, and it was then that he really started drinking heavily.

My dad's free-floating anger and drinking got worse and worse throughout my childhood. I never knew when he was going to fly into a rage and scream and get violent. I tiptoed through my life, and even though I tried to do everything right in his eyes, it was impossible. Inevitably, something would infuriate him, and any tenuous calm I'd manufactured by staying out of his way for a couple of hours, or at most a couple of days, would shatter. He was terrifying, and there were lots of moments he would have hurt me much worse than he did if someone—my sister, my uncle, my grandmother—hadn't intervened.

Perhaps now is a good time to explain why I call him Daddy. This was really not my choice, as was the case with pretty much everything in my life. He just always insisted on it; he liked it better than "Dad." I guess it sounded more endearing to him. I remember hearing someone at school call their father "Dad," so when I got home I tried it on for size. In response Daddy chewed me out, then completely ignored me for days. How utterly disrespectful I was for even suggesting such a moniker! He would be Daddy; nothing else was appropriate. I never made that mistake again—and even today, fifteen years after his death, I still refer to him as Daddy.

━ ━ ━

It wasn't until I moved out of his house that it was possible for me to begin to forgive him, which started with understanding him a little bit better. One thing that made it both harder and, later, easier to understand him was a conversation we had when I was seventeen. I wasn't living at home anymore, and the physical distance must have given me the courage to say what I said, and also might explain why he didn't become furious with me. Or maybe it was that he felt thoroughly defeated, in the face of his ongoing unemployment and being left by his second wife.

What I told him was this: I was sorry all this was going on, I loved him and always would, but I didn't like him. The look on his face was pure devastation. Now, as a mother, I can imagine how much pain I caused with those few words, though I don't regret saying them. He asked, "Why?" with incredible longing and sadness. And then I began to recount some of the awful days. I told story after story and after each one, he cried and said he just couldn't remember any of it. It made sense that he didn't remember: He drank from morning to night, in fact all through the night, since he was an insomniac. At the time, I was mad—these events shaped who I was, who I am, and he didn't even remember them. But now, so many years later, the fact that he was so drunk he didn't recall abusing me actually makes it feel a little better. It's hard to harbor anger at someone for things they can't even remember doing.

That was also when I first began to get a sense of his self-loathing—that he couldn't move past the mistakes he'd made and couldn't accept the man he'd become: an abusive, unemployed alcoholic. It would have been cruel not to grant him forgiveness.

Once I started to forgive him, I felt so much peace in my heart. The more I forgave, the more my anger about what he did diminished. It freed me enough that I could start my own life, separate from him, though he remained a part of my life until the day he died.

Someone recently asked me if I have also forgiven my mother. It's a hard question, with no straightforward answer. In part, yes, I do forgive her. But it's also not something I think about much. Basically, it's difficult to fully comprehend and forgive someone who has played such a shadowy role in my life. It's something I have to sort of make myself think about. For now, in the context of my busy, happy life, she is not in the forefront of my thoughts.

Mostly what I think about is that I never got to call someone "mom." If you, too, have never uttered that word to someone who adores you, you know what it's like: It sucks. When you grow up seeing this normal, everyday relationship at the center of all your schoolmates' lives, the fact that you never get to partake in it—that you never have a nurturing parent—it leaves a pretty big void. I remember always looking longingly at mothers and daughters who resembled each other and thinking how great it must be to know what you'll look like as you get older. That's probably why I'd get so excited whenever someone thought my sister, Serena, and I were twins.

I never got to have the normal talks many young girls have with their mothers, about boys or about my changing body. It wasn't until years after I first got my period that I found out about the existence of tampons; I will never forget that day. We were going to go swimming with our cousins and I realized I couldn't swim because I was having my period. My aunt Fatima took a tampon out from under her bathroom sink, unwrapped it, held it in front of the mirror and explained how to use it and how to dispose of it cleanly when I was done. I'm still grateful to Fatima for that.

I think more about my lack of a mom than I think about Patty herself. I do think about her sometimes, though—on Mother's Day, say, but only in that I wonder if she thinks about the children she left behind at least on that one day of the year. Who knows? In any case, it's pretty clear that she is not mentally sound. Abandoning your children—and it wasn't just Serena and me; she also had two boys, with different fathers, whom she left—is not something a sane, healthy person does. Being a mother myself, I know that you would just never do that unless something was really, really wrong with your mind.

Basically, I'm not sure I've ever felt enough for her to grant her forgiveness. It would be nice to feel more at peace about her, someday, instead of this vacancy I have in my heart. But I'm not sure if it will ever happen, given that she seems incapable of offering an apology, whether because of mental illness or something else. Is it possible to forgive someone who never apologizes? I really don't know the answer to that question.

I think about this sometimes, especially now that I'm getting older: How would I feel if I learned that she died? It's a strange thought. I'm not sure how affected I'd be by her death—and it's that fact itself that makes me sad. There is a hole in my life that will never be filled. Mostly, I have learned to live with that.

This absence in our lives was evidently glaring enough that even my dad, from within his fog of alcohol and rage, saw that we needed a mother figure, and that's how Karen became part of the family. Whether that was for better or for worse, I'm still not sure.

CHAPTER 2

Once, during high school, I asked Daddy, "Have you ever killed someone?" It was a question that most young girls would never think to ask their father. He told me the following story in reply.

Not long after Patty left us, he was getting ready to close up the strip club late one night, and two customers were getting loud and mouthy. I would guess they were getting handsy with the dancers too, but if so, Daddy left that part out. He asked them to leave; they refused and carried on being boisterous. He asked again, and again they ignored his request. So Daddy, always rational, hit one of them over the head with a beer bottle. The good news was they left the strip club and stopped being a menace to the strippers and other customers. The bad news was that when Daddy left the club, they were waiting for him outside, and one of them shot him in the stomach.

Daddy explained that, later, one of the men "killed himself" and the other one "disappeared"; that was all he said. He ended up making a ring out of the bullet they pulled from his stomach. It was the only ring I ever saw him wear.

Daddy realized that while he recovered, he was going to need more help than my uncle Hassan could provide, so he decided to find a woman to move in and help care for us full time. He chose Karen, who was a waitress at Dream Dolls. He thought she was the most normal of all the women there. He also probably knew she wouldn't ever challenge him on anything—he was her boss, for one thing; for another, she just wasn't the kind of person to stand up to anyone, on her own behalf or that of others.

She moved in with us when I was almost two—first as our nanny, but soon we were told she was our aunt, because she'd supposedly married Uncle Hassan, who was still living with us up to that point. The funny thing is, though, I don't ever remember Hassan living with us while Karen did. It's hard to imagine that Karen and Daddy were actually a couple: She would sometimes try to be affectionate with him, but he always acted disgusted by her and even said as much, pretty regularly.

To some extent, Karen did fulfill the role Daddy had in mind for her, cooking for us, dealing with my and Serena's daily routines of getting ready for school, sometimes making our school lunches if we were running late, taking us shopping for clothes before every new school year, things like that. She made sure we had toothbrushes and food in the fridge. She signed us up for after-school sports and took us to our practices and games. Daddy certainly didn't do any of the practical domestic stuff involved in raising children, except once in a while when he felt like cooking, and he also liked gardening. I don't remember a time before Karen, and I don't know what our lives would have been like without her. She did try to take care of us, in practical ways that were essential.

Daddy regularly beat and screamed at Karen, and I never saw her even attempt to stand up for herself. Nor did she try to shield us kids. She was a passive bystander to all of Daddy's screaming and hitting and neglect; she never once intervened, no matter how bad it got. In writing this book, I've realized just how much anger I have stored up in my heart for the role, or the lack thereof, that she played in all the madness of my childhood. I always focused so much on dealing with my anger toward Daddy, and I've even dealt a little with my anger toward

Patty for abandoning us. But I have never really dealt with my anger at Karen for her lack of action, which helped ensure for me a world of chaos and sadness for so many years. She stood by and watched all the violence in our home, and as a result, I trust people even less than I would have if we had just lived with Daddy—because, as the other adult in the house, she should have stepped in and tried to stop him. I never really believed that you could count on anyone. Once in a while, someone did step up for me, but it always felt like a wonderful bonus, not something I could expect.

I sometimes find myself reverting back to that mentality, even today. It's a form of self-protection, I'm sure—if I don't count on anyone, I can't be too disappointed when they don't come through. Of course, now that I'm an adult and have been out of my childhood home for so many years, I understand, rationally, that we don't have to go through life with that attitude. Today, I do all I can to make sure my monkeys—that's what I call my kids; more about them later—feel they can trust the adults in their lives.

Now, having done years of work with domestic abuse survivors, I have a better understanding of why women accept situations like that—why Karen stayed silent when Daddy hit us, and when he hit her. She came from a violent home herself, and, as so many abused children do, when she grew up, she got into a relationship with a severe imbalance of power and couldn't make herself leave, not for years and years.

I suppose my resentment of Karen was always about how she did nothing to protect me. But as a kid, I wasn't really conscious of that. I felt more hurt and angry about how she always did the bare minimum, both practically and emotionally. I guess it felt like an extension of Daddy's neglect. Birthdays were an especially strong symbol of how we felt unloved and untended. Every year, she made our birthday cake in a heart-shaped pan; she loved that pan.

Sometimes she'd try two layers, but it usually didn't work out and the top layer would slide to one side. It was like everything she did for us—slapdash and lopsided. And she loved wrapping our presents in newspapers. She thought she was being clever, but to me it just felt like she didn't want to go the extra mile and buy some wrapping paper. That's kind of how our birthdays felt in general: She did just enough, but there was no gushing about our special day. She always sang us "Happy Birthday" in this quavering falsetto—I hated it; it always felt so disingenuous, more about her amusing herself than about celebrating me or Serena. I wanted so much to be treated with love and joy on that one day especially, when most days I just felt in the way, at best. But at least she went through the motions, unlike Daddy; I can hardly remember him saying "happy birthday" to me during my childhood, much less singing the song.

To be fair, I should say that Karen always worked full time, which seems impossible, knowing her today. She didn't keep working at the club; she quit that job when she moved in with us, I suppose because Daddy didn't want the club to be part of his daughters' lives. For a while she worked at Peoples Drug Store and then at Bradlees (the Target of our day). She stuck with those jobs for a good long time. I'm sure she relished the chance to escape the house every day, even though she refused to leave permanently.

— — —

While in some respects, our dad watched my sister and me like prey, in many ways we were seriously under-parented. One of my earliest clear memories of childhood is from kindergarten. I can mostly laugh about it now, but at the time it was as terrifying as it was embarrassing. My only memories of the school itself are that it was at the intersection of two major roads, it had a big red door, and my kindergarten classroom had a bathroom with a door so big and heavy I was sure I would get trapped inside, everyone would forget I was there, and I would get stuck in there forever. I decided never to do battle with that door and instead thought if I just walked while I peed, no one would notice. When I thought about it after the fact, especially about the newspapers my teacher laid on the floor of the classroom and the spare pair of pants that were left for me in the front office, I realized that people had noticed. I have no idea what the school might have said to my dad or Karen about this behavior, but no one seemed to have thought it might warrant a conversation with a counselor. I guess school involvement in things like that were pretty different in the 1970s than they are today. They just kept replacing that spare pair of pants. Knowing all I do about child abuse now, I wish that someone at the school had looked into the reason I was so frightened of a door that I urinated on myself daily.

Thankfully, in the middle of that school year we moved to Springfield, a very pretty town. Big, strong trees and wrought iron street lamps lined the streets of adorable homes and lush green lawns. In spring and summer there were flowers everywhere. In winter, snowflakes fell in the glow of the old-fashioned street lamps. I was surrounded by peace and beauty in Springfield, and I think it contributed to my sanity.

We started at the local elementary school, Cardinal Forest, and I loved it. It was right by a small wooded area, in a beautiful little neighborhood. My kindergarten teacher, Mrs. Noss, was heaven. Pretty in a classic, all-American way, she was also kind and good. She took me under her wing; she was my closest friend in kindergarten. She was one of the lights in my life; I always clung to the memory of our friendship and wanted to grow up to be like her someday.

When you grow up without a mom, you don't get those simple nurturing moments where you feel safe and like no one will ever harm you because you have a Mama Bear looking out for you. In Mrs. Noss, for that one year, I got to feel that. For a long time, I kept a note she wrote me at the end of the school year; I remember it had little blue butterflies on it. I can still remember today the comfort and calm she brought me.

The other good thing that happened in my life when I was in kindergarten was that Daddy's mother, our grandmother Parisa, came from Iran to the States. Like Mrs. Noss, she provided me with a love and kindness that helped see me through the fear and loneliness I felt at home.

But, as was always the case in my childhood, the calm was upended by something new: I started experiencing what we called "weird days."

The first weird day I can remember occurred when I was in kindergarten. The whole school was in the hall for a cake walk fund-raiser, which was kind of like a bake sale mixed with musical chairs. All of a sudden, though I hadn't moved my feet at all yet, the entire school looked completely different to me, reversed almost. I realized that I had no idea how to get around the school—not to the front door, not even back to my classroom. It felt kind of like this: Imagine two identical model homes, the only difference between them being that they are mirror images of each other, so in one the staircase is on the left, in the other it's on the right. Now imagine that you're in the house with the staircase on the left, and you don't move or leave that house, but suddenly the entire house looks like the other house, with the staircase on the right. Now the kitchen is in a different spot; the rooms are all placed differently. You can, with effort, figure out how to get where you need to go by remembering the house with the stairs on the left.

That was the first of thousands of weird days; after that they happened on a daily basis. When they first started, it was hard for me to get a handle on them, and I would spend much of the day lost—in essence, in a weird haze. I would sometimes tell my family in the moments it was happening, and we started calling the episodes themselves "weird days", even though I would have multiple "weird days" every day. I soon devised strategies to deal with it. When it happened at school I would, for example, find my seat in the classroom by waiting until someone assigned to a desk near me sat down. If I had an episode at home, I'd have to concentrate on how exactly to get to the kitchen from my bedroom. If I was outside, especially going from one place to another, the whole town of Springfield would flip and look different. Certain roads were worse than others; the scenery would keep shifting.

Some days and moments were worse than others. Eventually, I figured out how to handle it well enough so that I was lost for only brief moments of time, seconds really, and then I'd "fix" it. I would put my head in my hands and really concentrate on figuring out what everything was supposed to look like so I wouldn't be completely lost. My sister and my cousin Saeed would laugh and mimic my head-in-hands routine, and Daddy would yell, "Stop it, Jessica. You're stronger than that; stop it!"

I would tell Karen and Daddy that I couldn't stop these episodes from coming and that I felt like this wasn't normal, that something seemed really wrong. I begged them many times to take me to a doctor. Daddy would repeat, "You're stronger than this!" And Karen would meekly shrug her shoulders and do nothing because God forbid she disagree with Daddy.

— — —

For better or for worse, Karen was around throughout my entire childhood, and many of my memories involve her. She always smelled like cigarettes and Jean Nate, that perfumed powder that was everywhere in the 1980s. She would get out of the shower and slather it all over her body without completely drying off, then walk around the house naked. She'd have patches of the powder on her body; it always bugged me—it seemed so lazy. It also bothered me that she'd ruin the powder's lemony scent almost instantly by lighting up a cigarette.

Karen never dressed stylishly; she was always casual, in Dr. Scholl's, usually paired with a casual non-descript cotton skirt. I remember thinking she must have felt out of place with all my elegant Persian aunts. But when she was kind, I always thought she seemed prettier than my aunts, because she wasn't as complicated as they seemed. Once she brought me home some pajamas just because she thought I'd like them. And she would often tell me I was beautiful and say she liked our pretty olive skin.

Once I became a mom, and even well before then, I started reading books on how to be a good parent: What skill sets were important to instill in your children. What lifestyles make for healthy children. How divorce and conflict affects them, and how you should try to avoid it at all costs. One of the common threads in all these books was how important consistency and routine are for children. All the chaos in my sister's and my life was compounded by living with a woman who often treated us indifferently and who was first our nanny, then our aunt, then our nanny again, then something else entirely (more on that later). Her presence was the one constant thing about her, really; she stayed all throughout our childhood, for fifteen years. And in the absence of an actual stable, loving parent, or of the mom that I always longed for, I developed such an allegiance to Karen that I maintained a relationship with her for years into adulthood—and for all those years, when she remembered to call on my birthday, she still sang me "Happy Birthday" in that weird falsetto!

With Patty gone, and Karen being Karen, and Daddy never in a million years dreaming of helping with any menial household task he didn't find enjoyable, Serena took on the brunt of parenting me. She was my little mini mama, which is ironic since we jokingly call my little girl that now, in part because she's so bossy with my son. But Serena really did have to take on the role of mom for me, and I adored and idolized her.

When we were really young, she used to put away my clothes. I think about that now, the pressure Serena must have felt. I see it all the time in the foster care world. The term for these kids is "parentified," and they don't really see a choice—they have younger siblings and they feel it's their responsibility to parent them, because the actual parents can't or won't. When I got a little bit older, Serena would constantly remind me to put my clothes and things away. She would come into my room and pick up a stack of magazines or a dirty shirt, which usually lay right beside a clean shirt—I always knew the difference, but Serena didn't appreciate this method of organization—and she'd say, "You have thirty minutes to clean up this floor or I'm going to come in here and start throwing stuff away."

As I write this I am laughing a little bit, and I also feel an awful lot of sadness. She shouldn't have had to be responsible for me, but she was. Serena is the person who taught me how to fix my hair and how to apply makeup. Of course, she was just a kid herself, and busy trying to survive in that crazy house, so some things slipped through the cracks—like what a tampon is, or anything about boys, or basic social skills.

When you grow up in an abusive, violent, broken home like we did, the dynamic between siblings is kind of strange. On one hand, you feel like you are literally all the sanity each other has. I remember one time Serena and I sat at the top of the steps crying and saying, "We are all we have, forever." But on the other hand, in a family like that, you're also kind of always fending for yourself; always having to watch your back, watch what you say, make sure you don't get into trouble; and you're doing whatever you need to do to survive. Serena drew a lot; that seemed to offer her sanctuary. I read magazines and books, spending hours imagining I lived in those houses featured in the magazines, or that I lived the lives of the characters in my books. And I wrote a lot, often about the family I wished I had. We each found our means of surviving, and oftentimes instead of joining forces, Serena and I withdrew into ourselves.

— — —

During these years, Daddy and two of his three brothers owned and operated a nightclub called Classics III. Sometimes we got to go there and sit in his office, and his cousin, one of our favorite relatives, would make us Shirley Temples. One time I remember dancing on the dance floor with its colored tiles that lit up. It was literally one of the only times my Daddy thought it acceptable for Serena and I to dance. And once, Serena fell at the club, splitting her knee open. I remember Daddy shouting at someone to get some alcohol and he opened the bottle and poured it all over Serena's knee. Serena always behaved as Daddy wanted, and so she didn't cry even though I'm sure it hurt a ton, and that made Daddy happy. They used to play commercials for Classics III on the radio; I liked that. It seemed cool that Daddy owned a nightclub and met bands and, I imagined, "rock stars." The best thing about the club, though, was that Daddy was gone a lot because he was working hard, and I liked the peaceful feeling in our home when he wasn't there. It was quiet and calm, without the nervous edge that always loomed when he was around.

I still carry a tiny smidge of guilt for this, but a lot of the time when I was growing up, I wished Daddy were dead. It made me feel evil and like God was going to punish me for thinking it as often as I did. But I couldn't help it. I just wanted him to go away. He ruined everything, made every day awful. When I would hear someone at school talk about their dad going on a business trip, I'd get so envious I'd literally feel it in my body, a physical longing for my father to go away, even for a few days here and there. Instead, because of an international crisis that happened thousands of miles away, Daddy lost the nightclub and started spending all his time at home.

On November 4, 1979, when I was in second grade, a group of Iranian students stormed the U.S. Embassy in Tehran, taking more than sixty American hostages. Looking at it as an adult, I see that that is trauma of such a different sort than I experienced, both for the hostages and their families; I simply cannot imagine the torment. But when I was little, I was more aware of this awful situation for the trickle-down effect it had on my family, though we were so far away from the actual events.

The students set the hostages free on January 21, 1981. I was in third grade by then, and while that was the beginning of a healing process for those poor people and their families, it was the beginning of the end for Daddy and his patience with people in general, but especially Americans. Somehow Daddy found a way to blame the American people for the fact that these irrational students thought holding a group of innocent people hostage was a good way to get their points across.

The hostage crisis definitely did make some people more suspicious of us, though, and in some cases hostile. A lot of Americans started to view all Iranians, even ones like us who lived in Springfield, as a threat. It became unwise to tell people you were Iranian, and from then on we referred to ourselves as Persian. My grandmother's house got egged. Worst of all, when people started learning that we were Iranian, so many customers stopped coming to Classics III that Daddy and his brothers had to close it down. As you might imagine, that sent Daddy even deeper into his spiral of rage and self-loathing. A lot of his fury during those years came from how people viewed us during the hostage crisis and even after it was over. Not only did I lose those quiet moments of peace I'd so enjoyed while he was at work, but the less he worked, the more he drank and the meaner he got, screaming and hitting as often as not. There were so many days and nights when it felt like it would never end. Like I was literally never going to escape that house and its madness.

CHAPTER 3

There was one good outcome of Daddy losing his business: When I was in fourth grade, we moved in with my gentle and loving grandmother Parisa. Or at least I assume it was because Daddy no longer had an income. He never discussed it with us; as with everything else, we were just told what was happening and what to do, and we did it.

I remember my childhood via the houses we lived in at different times. From kindergarten onward, we lived in the same neighborhood of Springfield, Virginia, always in pretty, well-kept homes that gave no indication of the madness inside. Before Grandmother Parisa's, we'd lived on Denton Court, in a white paneled house with dark green shutters. Later we moved to Carrleigh Parkway, into a brick townhouse with a deep red door and matching shutters. In fact, even when I finally moved out on my own, I lived just around the corner from Carrleigh. For now, we lived on Bridgeton Court with my grandmother, in a light-blue paneled house with darker blue shutters.

Ironically, right about this exact time, when it became extremely unpopular to be Persian, moving in with Grandmother Parisa meant that our life became even more Persian. My grandmother never learned to speak English, so we communicated in Farsi. I could never speak it very well, but I could understand a great deal, and still can. In any case, Grandmother Parisa and I found ways to communicate nonverbally. We understood each other without words most of the time, and I absolutely loved being in her presence, even if we were just sitting quietly. She brought me such a sense of calm.

Grandmother Parisa smelled like the thick Pond's cream she applied to her hands and arms many times a day. Her skin was like satin. She prayed throughout the day, on a little prayer carpet with stringy ends in her bedroom, and she would kiss a little stone as part of her ritual. When she looked at me, her eyes were always warm and full of love, though not smiling. There was always a deep sadness behind her eyes, and something else—concern, I think, looking back today.

She became our savior when we moved into her house. When Daddy had episodes, Grandmother Parisa pulled him off of me while Karen stood by watching, usually crying, her lower lip quivering, her chin all wrinkly. Nothing pissed me off more than seeing her make that pathetic face and act so cowardly as she watched my frail, five-foot-tall grandmother physically intervene before Daddy got in another slap or shove. Grandmother Parisa would have none of Daddy's rages; she would literally stand between him and the victim of the moment. She was the only person I had seen stand up to Daddy.

I sometimes tried standing up to him myself, but the results were always bad. One time I tried to get him to stop smoking, at least in the house. Marlboro Lights were such an enormous part of my life. That little plastic tab and the thin plastic wrapping pulling apart was something I witnessed on a daily basis. I can still sniff out a freshly opened pack of Marlboro Lights, even before one gets lit. And then there was the awful odor of the lit cigarette, the smoke filling our house and my lungs, which are still plagued with asthma and regular bouts of bronchitis today.

So one day when I had just had it with the stench and the smoke, I put up a sign in my daddy's room that said "STOP Smoking!" This little stunt did not go over as planned: He did not stop smoking. He did, however, get mad about it, berate me for nagging him, and stop speaking to me for the rest of the night. I never asked him to stop smoking again.

Moments like that, when I knew it was impossible to speak to my own father about what I felt, and that my opinion in the house meant nothing—those are the times that stick out the most, almost more than when he hit me. In all my years of public speaking about overcoming my past, people always cringe when I tell them about getting hit. But when I talk about emotional abuse, I don't think most people really understand that. I mentioned earlier that that kind of abuse was, for me, far, far more damaging than getting hit. Being ignored by Daddy was so painful, I still remember what it felt like, a hollowness felt into the depth of my being. I felt like a loser, like nothing; like if I disappeared, not a soul would care. Of course, it was his intention to make me feel that way—it was my punishment, very regularly, for voicing my opinions. I learned not only not to value my own opinions but, further, to keep everything to myself because, as Daddy told me regularly, all my thoughts were wrong.

I wasn't even allowed to say what I wanted to be when I grew up. He told me I should be a doctor or a lawyer, something respectable, and any other career was nonsense. What I really wanted to do was play the drums. Later, I learned it was in my blood: Patty's father, my grandfather Larry, had been a drummer in the Navy band. But drums were not for girls, I was told, and I would have to pick something else if I wanted to play an instrument, so I played the flute and hated every minute of it. When you grow up being told that every thought, wish, and desire you have is wrong—and knowing you'll be hit for expressing them—that damage lasts far longer than any bruise a fist might produce.

In general, though, I remember those years in Grandmother Parisa's house as the safest and most pleasant period of my childhood. Even though life with Daddy was its usual frightening and confusing mess, and he just seemed to get crankier all the time, having my grandmother around made everything so much better. Just eating dinner was a totally different experience when she was there. Looking at her kind eyes across the dinner table was such a comfort.

She also took care of us by cooking for us every day, delicious Persian food. While my friends were eating pizza and Hamburger Helper, I was eating ghormeh sabzi (beef cubes with kidney beans and spinach and rice) or loobia polo (green beans and beef and rice). The one challenge was that I hated cooked vegetables; still do. I never wanted to hurt my sweet grandmother's feelings, but she didn't seem to mind—in fact, she would pick out the meat and give it to me with rice and sauce. She always tried not to let Daddy see, when he ate with us, because she knew he'd get mad about it. I miss my grandmother Parisa so much.

Another reason those years were relatively happy for me was that we lived right next to the woods; there was even a creek hidden in them. Those woods were my sanctuary. I loved being there. I would sit and look up through the treetops at the patches of sky, and it calmed me and brought me so much peace. To this day, simply looking at a tree makes me breathe easier.

— — —

Sometime during this period, there was this big local news story about a crazed man who had cut off a police officer's ear. It wasn't your garden-variety assault, and the networks were going nuts covering it.

It turned out Daddy knew the culprit. Even then I knew it was backwards—Daddy was pissed at the police and acted like the cop had it coming to him. In reality, the poor guy was probably just trying to do his job, and his whole life changed irrevocably that day. I imagine there are lots of people like that out there, unlucky souls who bumped up against Daddy and his friends and paid a price for it.

In any case, Daddy's friend was put in jail for the ear incident, and for a while we visited him there fairly regularly. Or rather, Serena and I waited in the car in the jail's parking lot while Daddy went in and visited the guy. It's probably not a coincidence that years later, shortly after my daughter was born, she and I appeared in a public service announcement for a campaign called "Not Even for a Minute" about the dangers of leaving your children unattended in a parked car.

On the rare occasions Daddy brought us anywhere, jail parking lots weren't the only unsavory place he would leave us unattended. I remember more than once waiting outside of one of Patty's apartments. Yep, the Snake, my real mom, was still lingering about. Having purportedly split up with the famous singer, she was quasi-homeless in those days, and when she did have housing it was always in some unsafe, derelict neighborhood. Daddy still cared about her and would periodically go find her and give her money.

She also came to our house a few times and brought her shy, sweet young son along. True to form, she'd named him Hennessy, after the alcohol. He was about five years younger than me, her fifth and final child, the only one of us whom she raised, if you can call it that. His dad was not in the picture, and Patty didn't even let him see her parents; she was all he had, and she treated him terribly.

Hennessy—who now, sensibly, goes by Henry—and I keep in touch through social media and texts. I saw him on a trip to Virginia a few years back and introduced my family to him. Henry doesn't talk about Patty very much, but he's told me a few stories. One of the few times they saw our grandmother Elizabeth and grandfather Larry, Grandmother brought him a winter coat. Patty got mad because she said my grandmother should have given her money instead. Henry said he never felt like he could wear that coat because it made Patty mad. He also told me how she would lock him in his room from the outside and leave him for days at a time with a cooler of food and drinks. Yet in spite of enduring this unbelievable cruelty and neglect, he is a kind, sensitive person; you would never guess he lived with such a monster.

The few times we saw Patty she was loud, with a boisterous, frequent laugh. She smelled of cheap, musky perfume. Twice that I remember, she brought us gifts—gifts her friends in prison had made for us. Because while she didn't have time for her children, she did have time to visit several men in prison regularly. Two of her inmate pals made Serena and me jewelry boxes out of matchsticks. I kept mine for years, for some reason. My name was written in blackened matchsticks; in retrospect, I guess it probably took the guy a great deal of time to make.

I mentioned that outings with Daddy were rare and this was actually a good thing, because whenever we did get in the car with him, maybe to visit my aunts and uncles, he drove like he lived—like an out-of-control maniac. He would literally try to get up to 100 miles an hour on our little side streets, where the speed limit was maybe 25, just to see if he could go that fast without any other cars getting in his way. I vividly remember the fear, of course, but also something else—wishing for more, wishing we would crash and die so it would all be over.

⸺ ⸺ ⸺

Because I grew up lacking many pedestrian normalcies, being "normal" became a huge goal for me at an early age. It's why I was, without exception, drawn to friends with "normal" families. It was around this time, fourth grade, that I started to fixate on what I saw as the normal lives of other people—actual, individual people now, not just the ones I read about in magazines and books. As is the case with most dysfunctional families, we had a few "normal" days and moments scattered here and there, but mostly our life was anything but that, filled as it was with rage and chaos. And I yearned with my whole being for a normal life like my friends and classmates had.

I think it started with a project we did at school; we were making our own version of a yearbook for our class, out of construction paper. Everyone was supposed to write about their families, their homes, their lives. I remember holding the cornflower blue stapled booklet in my hands, eager to read all the mini biographies of my classmates. It was an inside look into the lives of all these people I desperately wanted to trade places with. And they did not disappoint: I got to see how everyone had parents—two of them who were married to each other!—one cat, one dog, one perfectly normal, happy life. All the other girls in my class talked about their dad's careers and their mom's special talents, like making the best chocolate chip cookies.

Then there was my little biography. I was so utterly embarrassed by how starkly different my life was from everyone else's. My biography went something like this: Jessica lives with her sister, her dad, her aunt (which is how we were still identifying Karen at this point, even though she had no apparent relationship with Uncle Hassan), and her grandmother. To my mind, the obvious translation was: FREAK! I also wrote that I wanted to be a doctor when I grew up; either Daddy had effectively brainwashed me or, more likely, I knew there was a small chance he'd see that little blue book and I didn't want to get in trouble for picking the wrong career ambition. Because I can tell you right now, I have never in my life wanted to be a doctor. The only way I would be okay looking at blood and guts and worse would be as a veterinarian, so all that awfulness would be overshadowed by the joy of playing with fluffy kitties and puppies.

Upon further reading, I did notice one other kid with an atypical household: Christopher Spinner lived with his dad and grandmother. I felt a little better that I wasn't the only misfit, but I always felt sad for Christopher because he lived in an old, run-down house off one of the main roads in Springfield, not really in a proper neighborhood like the rest of us. It was clear that money was not abundant in their household, so in addition to lacking a full, normal family, he also must have lacked some of life's simple pleasures, like new clothes at the start of the school year. One of the things Daddy and Karen did right was they made sure we had things like that; Karen would take me school shopping at the start of every school year and I got to buy Forenza shirts when everyone else did, and had a few pairs of cool jeans. I could at least make a show of normalcy.

During these years I started to make real friends, and I quickly realized how much happier I was when I was outside with them. I spent so much time with my friends in the woods behind that house or playing kickball in somebody's backyard. I got to laugh and smile when I wanted, and be the happy person I actually was, when I wasn't trapped inside our miserable home.

Better yet, I started to spend more and more time in my friends' "normal" homes. I always had friends with, as far as I could see, happy, loving, intact families. It's a huge part of what kept me hopeful, how I held on to sanity. My friend Sharon, in particular, had what felt to me like the perfect, happy family. Every time I went to her house, her mom was cooking something delicious, and she was always so kind to me. Sharon had a bunch of older brothers who were often around, and everything just felt so comfortable and easy in their home. It was what a family should feel like, and I relished being there and feeling like a part of it for a little while. I knew one day I would have children and make a happy home for us.

So far in sharing my story, I've tried not to bombard you with too much information about the effects of child abuse. But for a moment, I'm going to delve into a study on child abuse, because it's relevant to all our lives.

The Centers for Disease Control and Prevention conducted the Adverse Childhood Experience (ACE) study, which assesses the link between childhood maltreatment and later-life health and well-being. Anyone can take the ACE test. Your score basically reveals how crappy your childhood was and determines the likelihood of problems in adulthood. I scored a nine out of ten—the one test I've ever scored high on is the one where you want a low score! Because the lower your score, the better and more beneficial your childhood was. If you didn't have a lot of negative forces in your life, and unhealthy parenting styles thrust upon you, your score will be low. By contrast, the more adverse childhood experiences you had, the higher your risk for medical, mental, and social problems later in life.

I'm including it in the book (see Resources) because I want you to know your score. If you're like me and you scored really high but you live a pretty normal life now, you should be proud of yourself. If you scored really low, go call your parents and thank them not just for giving you an awesome childhood but also for giving you a leg up in life.

I have made lots of my friends take the test too, and it turns out they are all zeros! My two very best friends growing up: both zeros; my best friend here in Arizona as an adult: zero. My husband: zero.

I am very certain that in surrounding myself with zeros—people with blessed lives—I was able to counter my nine. I spent every day studying and loving and learning from the zeros and knowing that is what I wanted for my life.

It's funny, but that was only possible because of Daddy's neglect—I could be gone for hours at a time and he didn't care, as long as I was back when he or Karen told me I had to be. So, of course, I stayed away as long as I could.

Meanwhile, during the hours I did spend at home, I maintained a strange fantasy involving a specific bathroom in our house. I was convinced that while I was in the bathroom, it was going to separate from the rest of the house and fly away. The walls would remain intact, and the bathroom, which was now my home, would land in the middle of Africa. Fortunately, the plumbing would also remain intact, so I'd have running water, which would make me a hit with all the African villagers. I'd often bring all my magazines into the bathroom so I'd have something to do when I landed in the middle of nowhere. I also always brought my favorite stuffed animal. It's one of the earliest, and oddest, escape fantasies I can remember.

I kept striving for normalcy my whole life; I still do. It's why these days, on any given Friday night, I would much rather hang out at home, or at friends' or relatives' houses, and play board games or watch movies together than go out. Those simple weekend activities fill my soul with joy and love, and I look forward to them all week long. I always knew that if I could achieve normalcy in my life, I would have truly succeeded. And most days, I've done just that!

— — —

Soon after we moved in with my grandmother, we were informed that Karen was no longer our aunt and that we should once again refer to her as our nanny. It was a split-level house, and Karen's and Daddy's bedrooms were downstairs. Serena, my grandmother, and I each had our own room upstairs. That's partly why I liked living there so much—I felt safer being so separated from Daddy and Karen.

Then all of a sudden, when I was in fifth grade, we were told that Karen was going to move into Daddy's room because they had gotten married. No wedding, no white dress, no warning it was going to happen. We didn't understand it at all. From then on, we were to refer to her as our mom, though we never actually addressed her as "Mom."

While the official relationship between Karen and Daddy changed yet again, their dynamic remained essentially the same, just intensified. He yelled at her more, threw things at her more often, grabbed her by the arm more forcefully. Over the years, he bossed her around and it seemed to me that Daddy dominated her every thought, feeling, and action until she became a frightened, trembling nothing of a person who was unable to care for anyone, including herself.

When I think back on our family life, if you can call it that, I hardly remember doing normal family stuff like sitting around and watching TV together. And even then, we watched shows Daddy liked. Sometimes they were shows I liked too, like *The Odd Couple* or *Three's Company* (which we were never allowed to watch alone), but it was never fun because there was constant, monumental tension, and Daddy always got mad about something. Not to mention that I certainly wasn't about to laugh out loud at anything on the TV, because if he deemed the joke inappropriate, I'd get hit.

Once we were all watching TV together in the basement, and it felt as normal as it ever did, until Karen made a comment about what we were watching. I don't remember what she said, some casual observation, but it enraged Daddy, and he picked up a crystal ashtray that weighed probably five pounds and hurled it at her head. It just barely hit her—she was all right—but that was the end of that family moment. Daddy stormed out, Karen started crying as she always did, and just like every other time he got angry and violent for no good reason, we all just stayed quiet so as not to upset him further and retreated to our respective rooms, wondering what blow was coming next. Actually, come to think of it, I don't know where Karen went once she started sharing a room with Daddy. I just remember feeling sort of numb after incidents like that. I wasn't worried he was going to hit me next—when he was mad at Karen, he didn't usually turn his anger on anyone else. In this way, the constant worry and fear limited our interactions with one another. Writing this makes me really wish I had been kinder to Karen after this episode.

I don't remember any nice moments between Karen and Daddy—I never walked in on them sharing a moment alone, or having a private conversation, or giving each other a kiss or a hug. Daddy always acted like he hated Karen's very presence, which just added to my confusion over why they would marry. Nonetheless, I tried to see her as my mom, buying her Mother's Day cards and introducing her as my mom most of the time, which always made people do a double take. Here were Serena and I, two olive-skinned, dark-haired, dark-eyed girls, and our "mom" with translucent white skin, green eyes, and blond hair; we didn't share a single physical feature with her. When we introduced her as our mom, people always looked puzzled. Some would even say, "Oh, you guys look so much alike." I guess they were trying to be polite.

Karen and Daddy carried on like that for years, hating each other, Daddy always screaming at her, getting in her face, shoving and hitting her. He constantly put her down, calling her every name you can imagine, but she never once stood up for herself. She would stand there and take it, her bottom lip quivering, until he left the house, enraged at the mere sight of her. Then she'd cry and cry, and Serena or I or sometimes both of us together would go in and make sure she was okay.

— — —

We moved out of Grandmother Parisa's house just before I started seventh grade, when I was twelve. I was very unhappy about leaving; we were losing our defender and I knew we wouldn't have anyone on our side anymore. And it was true—things became worse than ever. Daddy didn't have to put on any kind of front once we no longer lived under Grandmother's roof. Plus, I didn't like the idea of her living on her own; she still didn't speak English and I just thought she'd be lonely. I also left behind my beloved woods, my sanctuary. It was the beginning of an especially painful and frightening stretch of years.

CHAPTER 4

I can't go any further in my story without talking about my maternal grandparents, Grandmother and Grandfather Littlefield. They were two amazing people, with a beautiful story between them. They met in a little neighborhood in Washington, DC, called Anacostia, at the intersection of Good Hope Road and Martin Luther King Jr. Road, as they told it. Later, when I was growing up, my grandparents lived in a beautiful town in Vermont, on Pleasant Street, which I never thought was a coincidence—everything about them, everything they represented to me, was pleasant. Both of them, and in particular my grandmother, brought me that beacon of hope every child, especially every abused child, so desperately needs.

My grandfather was in the Navy, and played drums in the Navy band, which is probably where my love of drums stems from. He said that the very first night they met, my grandmother grabbed him and kissed him. It startled him, for a couple of reasons: She was a girl, and girls weren't really supposed to do that in the 1940s; also, it was his first kiss. I love that story—how sweet were they?

About Patty, their first-born, my grandmother Elizabeth had this to say: She was always different, and she was a troublemaker from day one. Looking back today at the various stories I heard about her throughout my childhood, my guess is that she was suffering from some form of severe mental illness.

Patty had a reputation as the town slut. As a teenager, I was told, she slept with a few married men, and apparently one of those men got her pregnant. Patty thought she was going to raise that baby; from what my grandmother said, she didn't seem to fully understand the gravity of the situation. And then as quickly as she got pregnant, she lost the baby in some type of a fall. At least that's what she told my grandmother.

After the miscarriage, Grandmother Elizabeth said, Patty just got worse and worse. She moved out of town and they didn't hear from her for years. I learned later that Patty went on to meet another man, the next in a long string of entanglements, and she had a son with him—a son whom she quickly abandoned. Then she met someone else, and had another son, who also got left behind when Patty sought greener pastures.

Shortly after that little boy was left motherless, Patty met Daddy. She called her parents and told them she was pregnant and living with the father. They came out to visit; I still have the pictures. You can tell even from the photos how strained their reunion was. Even though there is a smile on my grandmother's face, I can see the tension in her eyes.

I remember my grandmother Elizabeth's eyes vividly, because whenever they looked at me, they were smiling. She looked at me with such love and affection and kindness. I always felt like the love Grandmother Elizabeth had for me was how I was supposed to be loved by a mom. She and Grandmother Parisa were the closest I came to that. Once, Grandmother Elizabeth told me she felt such guilt for raising a daughter who grew up to abandon her own children. And so when she wrote me, and when we spoke on the phone and especially when we got to visit in person, she always tried to impart all the life lessons that her own daughter didn't. We only visited them twice when I was growing up, but they came to visit us three times that I can remember, and maybe more than that.

My grandmother wrote to me about once a month; I still have some of her letters—in fact, I keep two of them, tucked in a Bible she gave me, on the nightstand next to my bed.

In her letters, she always told me how much she loved me and always would; I felt it so powerfully and unconditionally, and it gave me such strength. She would write about her love for God, and we talked about that on the phone a lot, too. I adored talking on the phone with her and my grandfather. First they would both be on at the same time, on different telephones. Eventually my grandfather would hang up, and Grandmother Elizabeth and I would keep talking. She and I had a bond I never had with anyone else. She was strong but kind, tiny but tough, and I loved her love of God and her belief in something bigger and better than this world. And, of course, I loved how much she loved me; it felt wonderful to hear those words from her and know she truly meant them.

Grandmother Elizabeth was also my idol growing up, because she lived her life fully and joyfully. She knew how to fly an airplane in the days when it wasn't acceptable for women to fly, and from what I'm told, she could land so easily you couldn't even feel it when the wheels made contact. She was the first woman assigned to make gears for car transmissions in a factory in Chicago, where they lived for a while. She taught herself to read music and play the guitar. She rode her own Harley Davidson until she got too frail.

I also idolized her because she loved her husband with all her heart. She and Grandfather Larry would slap each other on the butt and wink at each other; they were so deeply in love. You could just feel their love filling up any room they occupied.

Now that I live in the world of child abuse prevention, I know of countless studies showing that if an abused child has just one source of hope, one person who gives them guidance and love, who reaches out to them, they can survive and thrive despite the abuse. Grandmother Elizabeth was absolutely crucial to my life, in exactly that way. She was the role model I so desperately needed. She showed me that it was okay to speak your mind and be a strong, tough woman, but still be overwhelmed by love. She taught me to love and trust in God when every human being around me was failing me. She taught me to be the person I am today. I miss her terribly and I wish so much that she could have seen me as a mama. I know she would have been proud of the mother I am. I know she would have adored my beautiful babies.

⸺ ⸺ ⸺

Thank God for Grandmother Elizabeth's steady presence in my life, because, like I said, when we moved out of Grandmother Parisa's house, Daddy felt freer to be himself, and things got worse and worse. He started drinking even more and would spend many hours sulking and drinking himself into oblivion, watching Iranian TV or listening to his Persian music in the den. He also started shooting his guns in our basement, I guess as a stress reliever, though it stressed me out beyond measure. Daddy had a cabinet full of guns; they were his prized possessions.

I hate the sound of gunfire. My one positive gun-related memory was when we did target practice with Grandmother Elizabeth, shooting at cans with her gun. We were outside in beautiful Vermont, facing the forest with no other human around for miles, and no animal in sight, so I knew no one would get hurt. That seemed like a genuine stress reliever, and I kind of understood why people like to shoot guns, then.

Daddy would go into the basement, into a room with a thick cinder block wall that didn't share a wall with another townhouse because we were in the end unit. He had put some kind of covering on that wall, and he would fire the gun into it, again and again. If I got stuck down there when he was doing it, he would make me shoot too, saying, "It's good for you to know how to protect yourself, Jessica." The guns were powerful enough that they made me jump back a couple of feet. I hated shooting them. They were violent and loud and scary, just like Daddy.

Another thing he started doing once we moved out of Grandmother Parisa's house—I guess he didn't dare do it around her—was hosting opium parties. I'd come home from school to find the house full of men I didn't know, drugged out of their minds, talking in Farsi about how awful America and Americans were. I would head straight to my room and pray that none of them ventured upstairs; thank God, none of them ever did. That was the beauty of everyone being so afraid of Daddy; no one messed with him and thus no one messed with me—except him, of course.

Eventually, I'd get hungry and go into the kitchen, where often they would have left some of the opium out—they cooked it in tinfoil; it looked a lot like a Tootsie Roll. I'd grab a snack and run back up the spiral staircase to my room.

Another example of Daddy's combination of control and neglect: He always told Serena and me that we could drink or do drugs anytime we wanted, as long as we did it at home, in his presence. I remember the first time he gave me a beer. There's even a picture of it; I had to be in fourth or fifth grade: a girl with big round glasses and a snow hat on her skinny little head holding a Miller Lite. I drank some of it, but thank God I hate the taste of beer. I never took another drink in front of Daddy again.

Daddy also used to bring this homeless man into our house; I don't remember how he knew him. Maybe he was a friend of Patty's, now that I think about it. Daddy told us Tom's story: He came from a loving family, but he got involved with heavy drugs and they messed up his mind. He went insane, lost ties with everyone, and ended up homeless. I can picture him still—he wasn't a tall man, about Daddy's height, and he had white blond hair, blue eyes, fair skin. He could have been pretty normal looking at one time, maybe even handsome. Daddy called him Crazy Tom. Sensitive as ever.

Knowing how protective Daddy was of us, I'm guessing he threatened Crazy Tom's life if he even considered doing anything to us, and he never tried. Actually, I don't remember him ever looking at us like a predator would. Daddy made sure we were safe from him. And it was a real kindness on Daddy's part to take in this man who had lost his family, his life, his mind to drugs. Daddy would let him take a shower, give him a clean pair of clothes, and feed him. Then he'd put him in the car and drive him back to wherever he came from.

Remembering Crazy Tom calls to mind the fact that Daddy always had a soft spot for Patty, even though she had broken his heart, and even while her name would sometimes still come up in his drunken rages. In spite of that, he continued to seek her out, in increasingly destitute situations, and give her money. He always wanted us to talk to her and to forgive her. After visiting her, Daddy would occasionally bring us gifts from Patty—once he brought us these pink, heart-shaped glass necklaces, and once a dollhouse. I have no idea how or where she acquired these things. She also gave me a mug with "Jessie" printed on it; I still have that, actually. That, a few photos, and a couple of books she left behind are the only things I still have from her. I only know the books were hers because she wrote in them, and I recognize her handwriting. The older we got, the heavier and more urgent was Daddy's wish that we would forgive her.

And in recalling how Daddy could be generous and caring with people, I can't leave out the fact that he often went out of his way for his extended family. He often gave his mom and his siblings money. One time he even sold his beloved Harley Davidson motorcycle so that his brother could buy a car. He let his cousin live with us for a while, and he helped his sister in-law out when she opened a salon; things like that. I guess when his father died, he felt it was his responsibility to make sure his family was taken care of.

— — —

I am often asked how I survived my household with such a positive outlook, how I seem so "normal" despite my upbringing. One of my biggest coping mechanisms was that, starting in about seventh grade, I unknowingly practiced the tips from the book *The Secret*, long before it became a book. For instance, without any awareness of the law of attraction, I made my bedroom walls into one giant vision board, without ever having heard of that either. I cut pictures out of magazines of all the things I wanted in my life and put them up around my room. I had lots of photos of happy-looking families; I remember one in particular, a beautiful all-American family standing in front of a big pretty house. I would look at that picture and dream about the day I'd get married and have my own babies—that was always what I wished for most, creating a happy, normal life. I put up pictures of the car I wanted and the pets I would have when I lived on my own. And I put up the cover of a *TV Guide* with a picture of Miss America.

That was when I first started to dream about being Miss Virginia, and maybe even Miss America or Miss USA. I loved how articulate and strong and passionate those women were. They all had causes and goals and dreams, and they were all beautiful and fit. I just knew I would be on that stage competing in the Miss USA pageant one day. It must have seemed like the most insane dream to anyone I told back then—for many years, I was scrawny, with huge glasses, teeth too big for my face, and a mess of hair that I didn't learn to fix until I was nearly old enough to drive. But still, I longed for the day I would wear the crown and look as poised and confident as those women.

Those early "vision boards" are why I became so obsessed with magazines. I would kind of mentally insert myself into the pictures, and it was a powerful escape. In fact, thinking about it now, I see that I still use magazines as a coping mechanism today. I could spend hours looking at them! At a very young age, I knew I wanted to publish my own magazine when I grew up. On my bedroom walls I even put magazine covers like the ones I wanted to create one day.

I also practiced visualizing before I truly understood the word; I just called it daydreaming. My teachers would sometimes catch me at it and snap me back to attention, though not as often as you'd think. Now, in hindsight, I imagine all my teachers must have known about my family and cut me some slack. For me, school was about escaping home and being surrounded by my friends who loved me and made me feel safe; it was not about chemistry or algebra. I just wanted to look out the classroom windows at the trees and wish and dream about what I wanted my life to be.

I've always found it extremely calming to sit and look at trees. At home during middle and high school, I had a big tree right outside my window and I would sit and watch the leaves in the breeze and it just healed my soul somehow. There was also a playground near our house encircled by a group of old, tall trees. I would sit on a swing and put my head back and stare up at them, a little bit of sky peeking through the branches, and see my future self happy and smiling and feeling loved. I could see my children and my happy home, and my husband who would protect and love us all. Sometimes as I swung I cried about what my life really was, all the chaos and fear; I'd also cry in relief that, for that moment at least, I was free and looking at trees and feeling peaceful.

Something else that saw me through my childhood is that I've always focused on all the good in my life. As a kid, I made lists of all the things and people I was thankful for—my sister and my grandmothers and grandfather, and my cousin Saeed; whenever he was over, he was joyful and smiling, and my Daddy seemed happier and life seemed brighter. I was acutely grateful for my friends and some of their parents, for my teachers, for our pretty house surrounded by greenery, for the adorable cats and dogs we had over the years.

One thing for which I have always given thanks is my health, especially all my working body parts. I have never taken for granted that I have fingers and toes and arms and legs that work. All my life, I have often thought about how the simplest act, like picking up a glass of water, would be a huge feat for someone who has lost full use of their limbs. Or how lucky I am that no matter how bad a day I'm having, I can use my legs to walk outside, and my eyes to look at trees and friends and books and magazines, and my ears to hear the music that often served as a therapy for me. Even today, when my monkeys and I go to the store, we use the non-automatic doors; I used to say, every time, "There is someone who is wishing more than anything today that they could use their hands and legs to open and walk through this door, and as long as we're able to, we will use this door." I don't have to say it anymore; my kids just know, by now. I think my awareness of all the blessings in my life, including my healthy body, helped me not fall into despair as a child.

— — —

As Daddy's rages got worse and my sister and I got older, we started to intervene when he hit Karen. When he just screamed at her, without getting physical, we often just let it happen, because if we jumped in then, we became the target and it seemed kind of pointless after a while. But the hitting, that was too terrible; something had to be done.

Serena and I often asked Karen why she stayed; we urged her to leave and to take us with her. It felt odd, as a kid, to encourage an adult to make safer and better choices for herself and, by extension, for us. She'd always cry and say we didn't understand stuff like that.

It was around this time that I learned about Karen's own

childhood. Her family life was especially tragic and horrific: When she was a little girl, she watched as her father literally beat her mother to death. I cannot even imagine how terrifying and shattering that must have been, and my heart still goes out to the little girl Karen was so long ago.

Of course, at the time, I didn't make the connection between her childhood experience of violence and her choice in adulthood to stay with a man who beat her. But now, doing the work I do and knowing all I know about victims of domestic violence, I understand that she was following a path on which many abused children get stuck, in submitting to a cycle of abuse in adulthood.

These days, domestic violence victims are encouraged to come up with safety plans for leaving their abuser—plans that include short-term things like always having gas in the car and keeping a written list of phone numbers of important people, in case you lose your phone and need help; and longer-term things like keeping money and copies of important documents at a friend's house so that whenever you leave, you don't have to worry about some of the essentials for getting back on your feet. We never got that far with Karen.

I vividly remember one conversation I had with Karen after one of these episodes. Daddy had left the house, and she and I were in her and Daddy's bedroom. Now, of course, I see it with more perspective and subtlety, and more empathy—how survivors of childhood abuse can easily get trapped in abusive situations as adults and see no way out. But back then, as a child stuck in a life of fear and chaos, I felt mad at her and saw her as weak. I feel bad for that thought now, but at the time I could not understand her actions; it felt like a lack of love for us that she would "choose" to stay with him. I wanted Karen to leave him and to take me with her. More than anything, I wanted to get away from Daddy.

Another way things changed as we got older was that Daddy started being really strict about the way we dressed and wore our hair, and the tone of his criticisms changed: Beginning when I was about ten, he started calling me "slut" when he was displeased with me, which was whenever I was outspoken or boisterous. At first I didn't even know what the word meant, but his inflection and the look in his eyes told me it was not a good thing to be. He hurled the label at me with increasing frequency the older and more assertive I got; he called me a slut more times than I can count, because I couldn't keep myself from voicing my opinion. It's just who I am—even today, it's hard for me to keep my mouth shut when I disagree with something, especially if it seems unfair. I've always prized fairness and equality above almost everything, and both of those qualities were sorely lacking in our household.

If I wanted to wear a skirt, or paint my fingernails, or try out for the drill team in high school, I was a slut. One time there were these boots I thought were so cool; they had a tiny heel and looked kind of Victorian, all laced-up and gray. For wanting to wear boots like that, Daddy decided, I must be a slut. Sometimes he would say, "You're a slut just like your mother." Living with that kind of relentless irrational thinking takes such a toll on your mind; you just get so tired of your every thought and decision being scorned and shot down—it was utterly exhausting.

He called me a slut for wanting to shave my legs in junior high, and he forbid it. When you're born Persian, you get certain physical traits that are pretty great—skin that's "tan" even in the dead of winter, hair of a really deep, dark color, almond-shaped eyes. In America, Persians are considered quite exotic looking, a look most people like. But there's a big downside: the dark and plentiful body hair! Yes, Persians are a hairy lot, and the girls are not exempt. It does seem to have gotten better as I've aged, probably from so many years of waxing and shaving; in any case, I'm thankful because it isn't nearly as bad as when I was young. Or I suppose it's possible it wasn't as bad as I remember it, but when I was in junior high and not allowed to shave, I felt like I had baby gorillas attached to my legs. Wearing gym shorts with those legs did not boost my already low self-esteem—it was mortifying. So I was the girl in gym class who wore sweatpants even on a hot, humid Virginia day, because when you're thirteen, being hot in your sweats is a million times better than showing your hairy gams to the guy you have a crush on that week. No matter how much I begged to be allowed to shave those sweaters off, Daddy always replied with a resounding "No!" If I pushed too hard, he'd question my motives: Did I want boys to look at me? Why would I want that? "See," he would say, "you *are* a slut."

— — —

In our house, we did what we were told, moving and maneuvering around Daddy's moods. If he was happy, we were allowed to be happy; if he was mad, we knew to stay away; if he was sad—which always ended up looking a lot like mad—we knew, again, to steer clear and keep quiet. We didn't laugh or smile around him when he wasn't feeling it, because we would get in trouble. That's right: In my house, you would get in trouble for smiling and laughing.

I remember once sitting on the floor of the kitchen with a poster board and some books spread out in front of me, working on a map of some kind for school. For once, Daddy came by to see what I was working on. He read something out loud over my shoulder and, with his broken English, he said it wrong. I giggled, and promptly got slapped across the face. "Do you think that's funny?" he shouted. "Is that funny, am I funny? Do you want to laugh now, Jessica?" Slap. That was the end of my laughing on that night. Living with Daddy, it felt like I literally could never do anything right.

This irrational rule became one of those patterns of

emotional abuse that cast a very long shadow: I still don't laugh out loud nearly as much as I might. My initial response to something funny is not to laugh. Often I will just say, "That's funny." My children point it out every time we watch *America's Funniest Home Videos*. If I do actually laugh out loud, then you know you're pretty hilarious, because it takes a lot. But usually, even at genuinely funny things, if I can control my laughter, I do; it's just a reflex.

While I adhered to the no laughing rule as a way to stay safe, inside, I always tried to have a positive spirit—and I always tried to smile, as long as I didn't think Daddy was going to get mad at me for it. I don't know where my determination came from. And I came to learn that, if I was feeling really sad or mad but I forced myself to try to be happy and to smile, eventually I would actually start to feel happy. It made me feel like a crazy person the first couple of times I tried it, smiling when I was sad, but I kept at it anyway. I always think about that when I see pictures of abused children who can't even force a smile. I was at least able to fake it at times, but some kids can't fake it for even a moment, which shows the terrible depths of sadness in their little hearts.

All the time I spent dreaming about what my life was going to be like in the future kept me upbeat, for good chunks of my days anyway. It's interesting, at Winged Hope, the family advocacy nonprofit I started, we deal a lot with the issue of bullying, and it's made me think about my own childhood. I'm not sure if it's my spotty memory or if I'm really remembering this right, but I don't recall ever being teased or bullied. And now that I think about it, maybe I didn't get teased because all that visualization and positive thinking somehow caused me to exude an air of confidence. I surely wasn't built to own such confidence at that point, but I guess it's possible I seemed okay despite it all. I also managed to have some perspective on the madness of my childhood from even an early age—I always knew our home life was not normal, and I could even sometimes laugh at the nonsense of it all, even as a child.

God knows I was ripe for the teasing, with my hairy legs, my glasses, my puny physique, my hair that no one fixed, my weird family unit, and the fact that most of my family spoke the language of a country that the entire nation abhorred. But I don't remember anyone making fun of me. To have never received a tease or a poke about my crazy life or even about my appearance—it proves that mind over matter really does work!

CHAPTER 5

Like it does for all teenagers, during high school, my home life changed considerably. It didn't necessarily get easier, and to be sure, in some ways it got harder, as my friends and peers had the normal freedoms of adolescence while I still had to follow Daddy's narrow rules or risk getting hit or screamed at. It wasn't until my sophomore year that I was allowed to wear my hair down, though he still said only sluts wore their hair that way. Until then, he made me wear it pulled back. I couldn't even get my hairstyle right, in his eyes—and it wasn't like I wanted a Mohawk or something!

I recently found a stack of old journals I kept when I was growing up, most of them full of poems. They were pretty bad, from a literary perspective, but that wasn't the point—they were my private form of self-expression, so crucial to me all those years in Daddy's house when I was dying to express myself. All the things I wasn't allowed to say or to be anywhere else in my house, I got to be in my room, through my writing.

What I see in those poems is that, more than almost anything else, I was dying to be loved. Knowing what I do now about girls in abusive households, I see how likely I was to rush into marriage and start a family very young, had the "right" person come along. I could easily have jumped at the chance to leave my house and feel anything that even came close to love; many abused girls do exactly that. But thankfully that boy didn't come along until I was in my late teens and already out of Daddy's house.

My poems from my youth speak of hurting and longing and wanting to escape, which might sound like normal teenage girl drama, but it wasn't—it was desperation. I literally wanted to escape my house and, by extension, my life. I never once tried to run away, though, because Daddy said on a regular basis, "If you run away, go ahead, but you never get to come back." It shows that on some level he understood how awful he made our lives, and clearly a part of him was scared we were going to leave him.

But I did manage to get some independence during high school. It helped that I spent a lot of time at my two best friends' houses, more and more the older I got—especially at Sue's, which Daddy allowed because he really liked her. I went home with Sue almost every day during my junior and senior year. And by my senior year, when things between Daddy and Karen were really falling apart, I spent practically every weekend there—including after every school dance, which meant I got to stay out later and not worry about the end of the night. On those nights, the light, carefree feeling I took away from the dances stayed with me long after we left, because I didn't have to go back to my own home.

Being with Sue's family was such a relief, and a real blessing. They were so kind to me and to one another, and they were also the epitome of "normal," right down to their beautiful home. Sue's room was big, with hardwood floors, lots of bookcases, and a lovely window seat, which was my dream come true; I would sit there staring out the window at the trees and reading her books. We spent hours in that room.

Something pretty remarkable about my friendship with Sue—something I am only realizing as I write this—is that because she was so hilariously funny, and because I felt so safe in her house, when I was with her, I laughed all the time. In her house, I not only got to escape the unpredictability and terror of my home; I also got to escape my own inability to laugh out loud. No wonder her friendship has always felt like such a gift. We used to come home from school and watch *Oprah*, and Sue would make us Chex mix. I was in awe of how we were just allowed to wander around her house freely and uninhibited.

Daddy even allowed me to go on vacations with Sue and her family, and it was always heaven to get away from home for a stretch of time. For a few spring breaks, we went to Hilton Head Island in South Carolina. Sue and her family truly saved my life in so many ways; I was just so blessed to have them!

She spent a fair amount of time at my house, too, and even Daddy couldn't resist her—she had a terrific sense of humor; plus, she always treated him with a lot of respect. He genuinely enjoyed her. Sue and I were talking about my childhood recently (she is still a big part of my life) and she said that, in retrospect, she's surprised she wasn't more afraid of him, that in fact she was pretty relaxed around him, even knowing all she did about him. He did have a soft side, and the people outside our immediate family generally got to see it more than we did. And he was especially warm and relaxed around Sue. She knew how terrifying he could be—I had told her everything, starting in around ninth grade when we got close—but it was clear he was never going to act that way when she was around.

Daddy always used to make Sue try different Persian foods; I think he thought it was funny how much she did not want to try them. He'd make her drink this yogurt drink called Doogh, which I love, though I have yet to find anyone not of Persian descent who can tolerate its strong taste. I think it scared Sue off yogurt for life!

Sue even slept over a handful of times, which gave me some of the normalcy I always craved. She and I have since talked about how we can't believe her parents let her spend the night, since they knew my family life was crazy. I remember feeling thankful to them, even at the time.

I'll say it again: thank goodness I always had friends. But though I didn't realize it then, now I imagine that I was probably "that" girl during my school years, the odd one no one could quite figure out. I didn't fit in with the popular group, though I was friendly with some of the kinder kids who were popular. I wasn't outgoing, but I wasn't an introvert either, and I had my own set of friends. On my bad days at home, I'm not sure what I was like at school, probably a lot less patient with everyone. I always tried to keep the smile on my face—still do—but I suspect now that lots of people probably knew something was not quite right behind my smile.

Because things still really were not right, even with my newfound independence. Whenever I was at home, Daddy was as scary as ever. When I was in tenth grade, I blew off the advances of this boy at school who liked me; he even gave me a gold bracelet (which he had stolen, I learned later). To get back at me, he and his friend prank-called my house—God knows what they said to Daddy. I came home from a normal day at school and when I walked through the front door, Daddy was waiting for me. He marched over and slapped me in the face, screaming, "SLUT! Why are you such a *slut*, Jessica?" I had no idea about the prank call at this point; as far as I knew, he could have been angry about the color of my shirt—you never knew what would set Daddy off. He just spat something incoherent about a phone call from some boys.

Later that night I heard from my cousin Saeed and from Sue which boys had called the house. The next day in school, Saeed and a couple of my male friends (Daddy, of course, knew nothing about them) decided to beat those two boys silly that afternoon. Some teachers got wind of the big brawl that was about to happen, and that was my first trip to the principal's office. I remember sitting at a big conference table with Saeed and these counselors and the principal and some other school staff, and they asked us what was going on. When I finished telling them the story, they decided not to punish Saeed and my friends and let it go.

At that meeting, no one addressed the fact that Daddy had hit me, which they all knew about, because they insisted on knowing why this fight was being planned. The school counselor talked to me about it afterward, and she was very compassionate, as always. But nobody reported the abuse. I feel incredibly mixed about that, now that I work in child abuse prevention. At the time, I was so thankful that she never told, because I didn't want to be removed from my home. Yet, lots of kids would be better off if they were taken out of their abusive homes. In any case, I don't hold it against that counselor now, not at all—and it certainly shouldn't reflect poorly on her; things were just so different back then. Anyway, the situation got cleared up at school, but at home I was still a slut.

— — —

During my uber-tumultuous high school years, my quest for a normal a life outside our home intensified: I attended proms and homecomings. I went on double dates and to parties, and I tried very hard to experience as much normalcy—and as much life outside of and different from my own—as I could.

It's why I joined the Children of Alcoholics group my senior year in high school. I liked COA in that it was nice to learn I wasn't the only one with an alcoholic parent and a chaotic home life; it made me feel less lonely and freakish. But I also remember sitting in those meetings and wishing I had the parents some of the kids talked about. When someone said, "My mom's always passed out on the couch," I'd think, "I wish Daddy would pass out, or even just go to sleep for God's sakes!" That man was always awake, and always drunk and mean. Another student's dad was a goofy kind of drunk who would embarrass her by acting silly. There was even a girl with a boyfriend who was already a drunk in high school! She was a lovely person, and while I felt bad for her for being so sad and anxious, at the time I couldn't help thinking, "Ummm, you don't have to be with that guy; it's not like you live with him and have to endure his nonsense day and night like the rest of us do with our parents." Now that I'm years out of my abusive childhood, I understand better how people can suffer in different kinds of ways. I wonder what happened to that girl, and to that guy who was already an alcoholic at seventeen.

One of the weirdest parts of COA was that after the meetings, you'd pass these same people in the hallway— people you had just shared your deepest, darkest secrets with, and because none of them were in my circle of friends, I couldn't even say hi to them. My friends would have wondered how I knew them, and because of the group's strict anonymity policy, I wasn't allowed to tell. So you'd open up your heart to someone, and them to you, and then an hour later in the lunchroom you'd completely ignore each other. It was very strange.

— — —

The main way I got small measures of both normalcy and freedom as a teenager was by getting a job. Daddy didn't want me to work while we were in school, another one of those "just because I said so" rules. He said he thought it would affect our grades, but the truth was I had always had terrible grades. I got my first "D," in social studies, in the fifth grade. For me, school was always about being away from home, about my friendships there, about watching how "normal" people behaved; it was about everything but the subjects I was supposed to be studying. And I rarely showed Karen or Daddy my report cards, especially during my last two years of high school. They were going through so much in their relationship at this time that my grade in geometry was the furthest thing from their minds. So Daddy's argument that jobs would affect our grades was unconvincing. I'm guessing he just didn't want us in the real world, because he had seen how crazy it was and was worried we'd be drawn to the same crazy life he lived.

But, talker that I am, I convinced Daddy I should get a job, and thank God for Sue; she helped me convince him it would be okay if I worked. In fact, my first two jobs were thanks to Sue and her family. Her parents helped us get interviews at a fireworks stand—where we earned some serious cash and had a lot of fun every summer from the time we were thirteen—and then at an animal hospital, where we started working during the fall of ninth grade. I loved working there. We were receptionists for three veterinarians, one of whom, Dr. Umber, was one of the funniest people on the planet. Sue and I were friendly with a couple of boys who worked there, too. Over the years I became good friends with one of them, Pat, who gave Dr. Umber a run for his money for being the funniest person ever; he and I dated, too.

When the funny and very kind Dr. Umber and one of the other veterinarians bought their own animal hospital, I went with them. Dr. Umber was another one of the adults in my life who showed me that there were better, happier ways to live; he became a true friend. Besides making me laugh constantly, he was one of the first people outside of my circle of friends whom I told about Daddy hitting and screaming at me, and he always listened with kindness and concern.

I'm so thankful for every one of my jobs growing up. It was one more avenue for me to see the world as it could and should be, and not how it was in my chaotic home. It was a chance for me to meet hardworking, intelligent, motivated men and women. I just didn't have that kind of role model in Daddy or Karen. I feel mean saying that, but it's the truth. Maybe Daddy was smarter than I give him credit for, but it's hard to find the intelligence when it's blurred by a lifetime of Smirnoff.

— — —

There were still lots of ways Daddy controlled me, though, or tried to. It was not okay with him that I had black friends, for instance. I got hit many times for standing up to him when he said racist things about them. I remember getting in lots of trouble once when I got a ride home from school with one of my guy friends who was black. In addition to hating how racist he was, I couldn't help but think that maybe if Daddy wasn't drunk all day, and got his butt off the couch to pick me up from school, I wouldn't have needed that ride!

Probably Daddy's most dramatic attempt to "protect" me took place at the wedding of a second cousin, when I was in tenth grade. My pink lacy dress covered up most of my body, something Daddy insisted upon. But by then my sister and I were at least allowed to wear our hair down and to use hairspray and other products—not a big deal for most girls, but momentous for me.

We were all having a really great time at the wedding, as we often did when we were with our extended family. There was the usual yummy Persian fare, and we were dancing and having fun with our cousins. Apparently, a guy who was older than me—but not very old, maybe early twenties—was checking me out. I remember dancing and then all of a sudden Daddy showed up in a rage, grabbed Karen by the arm, and said we were leaving immediately. I found out later from someone in my extended family that Daddy had seen that boy looking at me, and he was not happy about it—so he stabbed him and told him if he ever looked at his daughter again, he'd be dead. I assume—and hope—that it wasn't a very serious injury, because the police weren't involved or anything. But it's still a really extreme response to ogling!

It's strange, because even though Daddy instilled more fear in me than any other person alive, I also always felt completely safe from other men throughout my childhood and adolescence. I knew if anyone ever messed with me, or even thought about messing with me, they might literally get killed for it. There was a safety in that, amidst the fear. Once, after high school, I ran into a former classmate, and he reminisced about the rumor around school that if you came to my house, there was a great chance you would be chased off by Daddy with one of his guns. It was a rumor for a reason: It was not far from the truth!

— — —

Serena graduated from high school at the end of my sophomore year, and I couldn't bear the idea of living in that house without her. I was so stunned and distraught at her graduation that I barely even registered the fact that Patty was there, with Hennessy in tow. Out of the blue, she'd asked if she could come, and Serena reluctantly said yes. But it was the least of my worries that day.

All through junior year, I spent most of my time out of my house—at school, at work, and at friends' houses. I got through, but things felt even scarier and more hopeless than they had before my sister moved out.

Then there came a day that changed and spared my life all at once. The argument started with me defending Oprah Winfrey when she appeared on the television in a commercial for her show, still new at the time. As he had done many times before, Daddy called her a "dumb ape." Usually when he said slurs—like muttering the n-word whenever we saw a black person—I would just say, "Daddy . . ." in a tone that implied I didn't approve. He'd give me a dirty look and say, "Someday you'll understand," and then we'd be done talking about it. But on this particular day, it really bothered me. It was becoming clear by then that Oprah Winfrey was a pretty amazing human being, doing her part to make the world a better place for a lot of people, and I felt the need to stand up for her.

So I did the unthinkable: I told Daddy off. I said, "I'm tired of you calling her that; she seems like a wonderful person and she's a human being. You need to stop calling her that!" Before I could go on, he slapped me hard across the face. I don't know what it was about that moment, or that slap, but I'd had it. For the first time in all my seventeen years, I hit Daddy back. I balled up my fist and, for every hit, slap, and shove; for all the hours and days I was ignored and demeaned; for all the nights I slept lightly, listening out in case Karen got hit; for all the nights I buried my face in my pillow and cried until it was so wet I had to flip it over; for the fear I felt every time he shouted at me; for the pain of never feeling loved and wanted; for the sadness I felt every single day in that house—for all of it, I punched him square in the face.

Daddy literally picked me up and threw my body to the ground, which was not an easy feat, since by that time I was already a little bit taller than him. But he was always very strong. Then, before I knew what was happening, he was kicking me in the ribs and the face, and I was fighting back and dodging every kick I could. Within no time Serena, who was home on summer vacation, was down there with me—you learned to keep an ear open at all times in our house, in case you needed to step in. Karen was nowhere to be seen; when Daddy got violent with us kids, she usually went into her room. I managed to get up and dodge him, and with Serena trying to hold him back, I ran up the stairs and into the kitchen. Once there I stopped for one of those moments that in reality is about two seconds but feels like an hour: I saw the butcher knife on the cutting board, and I saw the telephone on the wall in front of me. I went toward the knife first, and for a moment, I seriously considered using it—considered ending him, and ending the fear and sadness he perpetuated with his every breath. But then I decided to call the police and so I lunged instead toward the phone, passing by a large window behind the kitchen table to get to it. Before I reached it, Daddy was upstairs and Serena was screaming my name. When I turned around, I was standing right in front of that second-story window. Daddy picked up our kitchen table and threw it at me, and I don't know if the freak strength I summoned at that moment was brought on by adrenaline, or God, or both, which is what I like to think, but somehow I caught that heavy oak table in my hands.

He didn't stop even then; he kept lunging for me. I ran back downstairs but he caught me and knocked me down again. Now I was pinned up against a sliding glass door and couldn't get away from him, and then he kept kicking and punching me for a long time. I dodged as many blows as I could, and after what seemed like forever, when I'd grown exhausted physically and emotionally, and my body was about to quit the fight, Uncle Hassan appeared and pulled Daddy off me. Karen or Serena had called my uncle at some point, and Daddy was beating me up for so long that Hassan had time to drive over from his house.

Uncle Hassan dragged Daddy out of the house and drove him away somewhere, and in the quiet after his raging, I was absolutely beside myself. I was so pissed off, and so sad, and so tired from running all over the house and trying to fight Daddy off, and also just tired, throughout my whole being, from all the years of hitting and screaming. I was tired of feeling like every day was a crapshoot to see who was going to get hit, and who was going to get ignored, and what I was going to be in trouble for that day. I was tired of never being allowed to say what I thought or felt. I was tired of not getting to be who I wanted to be and do the things I wanted to do because he said they weren't appropriate. I was tired of the opium parties and the creepy guys in our house. I was tired of defending Karen, of telling her this wasn't any way to live, of trying to talk her into leaving. I was tired of wishing for something better for so long and still waiting for that wish to come true. Seventeen years is a long time to wait when you're living it—it feels like an eternity.

I was in my room alone. I'd closed and locked the door, which was not allowed, but what was he going to do, beat me some more? I was crying, desperately frustrated, when I remembered the bottle of pills I had stashed behind my dresser mirror. I don't remember where I got them—I assume they'd been prescribed to Karen or Daddy for something and they hadn't finished them—and I don't even know what they were, probably antibiotics or something that wouldn't have even done the trick. But in that moment, I decided I was ready to be done. In that moment, it felt like there was always going to be more sadness and fear than peace and happiness. Normalcy seemed as far away as ever. And so I took the bottle and poured the little red capsules into my hand. Right then Serena, in some kind of instinctual sister-moment, started banging on my door and demanding that I let her in.

I opened the door, pills in my hand; clearly I wasn't as serious about committing this act as I'd thought I was a moment earlier. Serena was devastated, and so mad at me. She called Karen in, and this time Karen actually seemed to care, and she said that she was done: She was going to leave him, and I wouldn't ever have to live through a day like that day again. It was a promise she actually kept, and within a few months, Daddy moved out.

Somehow, that night all I had to show for the fight was a couple of broken fingernails and a little bit of a black eye. That, too, must have been God's intervention, making sure my wounds weren't as serious as they should have been—either that or I'm just a UFC fighter in the making. That wretched day was the last time anyone has ever hit me. It's a fairly unusual claim, but it's true: The only fistfight I've ever been in was with my Daddy because for the remainder of the time he lived with us, he tried harder, he stopped drinking for short stints, and he never hit me again.

— — —

Even though I still carry anger toward Karen, as I've gotten older, and deeper into abuse prevention work, I've come to understand her better and to feel sympathy for her. It's pretty clear why she was the way she was—after growing up with a violent, alcoholic father, she was unable to "break the cycle," as we say in the world of child abuse and domestic violence prevention.

Karen's father served some time in a mental institution for murdering her mother, but he was a free man for the majority of his life. Karen did not speak to him for decades, until the day she heard he was dying from diabetes and was about to lose his legs to the disease. Daddy told Karen she had an obligation to take care of him. They had long conversations about the money he was going to leave behind when he died and how Karen was more likely to get that money if she was kind to her dad in his final days. And so it happened that a mean, legless, dying murderer was moved into our finished basement. His hospital bed took up half the space.

Our laundry room was in the basement, so I had to go down there regularly. I knew that he had killed Karen's mother, and I was pretty freaked out by his presence in our house. I would run as fast as I could up and down those stairs, with a quick, "Hi, how are you," and "Bye, I have homework to do." Once, touching the bandaged stumps of his legs, he said to me, "I like to listen to you running up and down the stairs."

Karen barely talked to him while he lived in our house. The only person who did was Daddy, but not much. It must have been such a lonely way for anyone, even a monster like him, to spend his last days, trapped in a hospital bed in a stranger's basement.

One day I was on the phone with Sue, talking about the boys we liked and what we were going to wear to school the next day, super important stuff like that. She was used to my Daddy by now. Though he was always on better behavior when other people were around, she came over often enough that she saw sides of him most other outsiders didn't have the pleasure of seeing—when, for instance, we were on the phone and Daddy needed it, he would pick up the receiver and shout, "Jessica, get off the PHONE!"

He did this so often that on this particular day, Sue and I just kept talking; it wasn't worth ending our conversation if he didn't really mean it. But then he did it again, louder, and Sue asked if maybe we should hang up. "Nah," I said, "he'll forget about it." Then a third time: "JESSICA, GET OFF THE GODDAMN MOTHER F-ING PHONE NOW!" We hung up that time.

It turned out Karen's father was having chest pains, and Daddy was worried he was having a heart attack—he was, and it killed him shortly after the ambulance took him away. It was probably the saddest funeral ever, with fewer than five people in attendance, all from our family. He appeared not to have had a single friend. His own son, Karen's brother, didn't even come.

Karen seemed sad that day but in a strange, disconnected way; it was almost like she was acting sad because she knew she should. It must have been confusing to "lose" the person who had killed your mother. I saw her cry once, though I think it was more because Daddy was bothering her than due to grief. The moral of the story is this: Don't beat your wife to death; no one will come to your funeral and no one will cry over your grave.

— — —

One day, soon after Karen's dad died, I was up in my room when I heard Daddy yelling at her. Having inherited some money from her dad, she had recently started grumbling about leaving, and Daddy was becoming really insecure and nervous. They argued for a while and then he shouted, "I'm just going to kill myself! I'm going to shoot myself right now!" It was not the first time he'd threatened to kill himself, but his suicidal talk had gotten more frequent and serious since Karen had started talking about moving out. Thank God Serena was home for a visit, and she and I went downstairs and were immediately dragged into the middle of the fight. They were both shouting at us, giving their respective sides of the argument, and then Daddy said again, "I'm going to end this and kill myself right now!"

This time he headed into the den, where his gun cabinet was. Serena, Karen, and I just stood there in the kitchen for a second, and then Serena ran after him, shouting back at us, "Aren't you going to stop him?" I honestly had no intention of running in there after him; he had been threatening to kill himself pretty often, so I was kind of numbed to it and didn't really believe him. I thought he was just saying it to try to keep Karen from leaving. But when Serena went after him, I was scared for her, so I went too. I saw Serena struggling to get one of Daddy's big rifles out of his hands. I ran back to the kitchen to call the police, but before I could get to the phone, the gun went off. For that moment when I didn't know who might have been hit by that bullet, my life stopped. Then Daddy ran out of the den and Serena came chasing after him, and my heart started beating again.

I heard sirens approaching after Chris called the police. Before we knew it, Daddy was literally on the run from the police. Shaken, Serena and I sat on the bottom stair, and she told me that the gun had fired into the closet as she struggled to get it away from him, Daddy's gun cabinet was not only full, it was full of loaded guns. Karen answered the door to the two police officers, and we took them into the den to show them the hole from the gunshot; then we told them the whole story. They said they would wait there a while because they assumed, incorrectly, that Daddy would return shortly and they wanted to talk to him.

Serena and I sat where we had a good view of the front yard so we could see if Daddy was coming back. As we waited, we heard the two police officers admiring Daddy's gun collection. We looked at each other in disbelief; two more on the long list of disappointing adults encountered so far.

But once again, Grandmother Elizabeth came through, with a letter that meant so much to me. I still have it; it's dated July 21, 1991:

Dear Jessica,

I enjoyed our talk Sunday, it was especially nice with no one rushing us. I wish the topics could have been better. These are bad times for you and I know that you will find yourself changing in many ways. Don't ever lose faith in yourself and remember that none of this is of your making. And whatever your Father is doing now or does in the future is of his own choosing. May God bless you and keep you always. We will be talking again soon. Grandfather sends his love & we are always here for you.

We love you dearly,
Grandmother

It's one of a couple of letters from her that I keep in a Bible, by my bedside.

— — —

A couple of years after high school, I ran into a guy from my class who said, "Oh yeah, you lived in that corner house that the police were always in front of." That was pretty embarrassing. Apparently, the police came to our house with some frequency, though I only actually remember a handful of times. Every time, Daddy took off before they got there, so we were left explaining the situation to the police. Once that I remember, they showed up because Daddy had a hit-and-run car accident; as far as I know, no one was injured, but I'm actually not certain. As usual, he wasn't home when the police came looking for him. In fact, he didn't come home for a couple of days that time, but the police never came back. And I remember the police just showing up after one of Daddy's rages—none of us had called them, so I guess a neighbor must have. That day, and all the other times the police came to our house, I never remember seeing our next-door neighbors, except for a couple of ladies across the street who would come out and watch. I'm sure our house offered plenty of excitement.

I was always surprised that our neighbors didn't call the police more often. I imagine they were probably as afraid of Daddy as we were. They had to have heard the gunfire when he did target practice in the basement. Since we were the end unit in a row of brick townhomes, we only had to worry about a neighbor on one side, and I wouldn't be surprised if Daddy had paid them a visit when we first moved in to "encourage" them to mind their own business. In any case, they certainly never came to our rescue, which is what we are now trying to teach people across Arizona to do, to intervene in a safe way. The current prevention wisdom is this: If you know, or even just believe, that a child or an adult is being abused, be their voice and report it. Many of them are praying every night that someone will.

I want to be so careful in addressing this issue of removing children from an abusive home. I know a lot of people feel confusion about whether or not it's always the best thing to do, because of the dangers children face in some foster homes, and I can certainly understand their concerns. But here's how I feel about it: I can see it from both sides, because I've been on both sides.

From the child's perspective, I understand, 100 percent, wanting to stay with a family and a parent who abuses you—because it's not like you stop loving them. There's an expression in our world, "Hate the abuse, not the abuser." That's how it often feels for these children who are removed from the only homes and families they have ever known. When you're a kid who's living it, that's your reality. And while it's an unhappy one, it's still the only reality these children know. When I was a kid, I didn't want to be taken from my home and my family to go live with strangers who might have been worse than Daddy. When I saw that Patty's neglect and emotional abuse would have likely been worse to live with than Daddy, I learned firsthand that the evil you know is better than the evil you don't. So I was relieved the counselors at school never told the police—though I'm not sure they would have done anything back then, anyway. In today's world, I would have been removed for sure.

But as an adult in the world of child abuse prevention, I know that, in many cases, these children's lives are at risk when they stay in their homes. In my own house, I could have been accidentally shot on more than one occasion. I've met an amazing survivor who was shot at age seven in her home during a fight between her parents; she's lived her entire life since then in a wheelchair.

I think it's my ability to see the situation from all angles that makes me effective in my line of work, and in my volunteer work, especially with the foster care review board on which I serve. I can absolutely empathize with the children who want so desperately to stay in their homes, no matter how much trauma they are witnessing or experiencing. But as a parent, and an advocate for children, I know that no matter how much these children might want to stay, in so many instances, they simply cannot because their lives are at risk. So if you know or suspect abuse is happening, even if you know the child loves the abuser, you need to report what's going on. It could literally save the child's life.

I want to mention a bright spot here: In my child abuse prevention work, I have encountered some amazing police officers, people who make it their life's mission to help abused children and who wouldn't dream of being so insensitive as the officers who had been to my home on those scary days. I'm beyond thankful for those officers who fight for the children who can't fight for themselves.

CHAPTER 6

Not long after I caught the kitchen table Daddy threw at me, Karen decided we should stage an intervention with Daddy. He was already onto the fact that Karen might be leaving him and he was in a panic. He attempted to quit drinking, but we knew he was hiding his vodka in the toilet tank in the basement bathroom, hoping we wouldn't venture in there. Karen got the idea that if we convinced Daddy to get help for his drinking, he really might be able to stop once and for all, in which case she would think about staying with him, which is very common in domestic violence situations. The abused woman wants to believe she can "fix" her man and she tries to give him every chance to change. It takes an average of seven attempts for a victim of violence to leave their abuser.

My memory of the intervention isn't nearly as clear as my memories of some intervention shows I've watched on television; as with other aspects of my childhood, family strife centered around addiction has always seemed to capture people's imaginations—it turns up on TV all the time! I remember that we did our intervention in a very public place; it might have been a food court or a hospital cafeteria. We had a counselor on hand to help us, someone I'd never met before and he left no lasting impression. He seemed just to be going through the motions, like we were just another case for him; I didn't feel like he grasped the severity of our situation or cared about our family.

Despite the counselor's lackluster performance and Daddy's

minimal participation in the intervention, he did agree to go stay in a hospital psych ward; he went immediately. Of course, he hated it. He didn't understand why he was surrounded by crazy people, when he was trying to get a handle on his drinking. He soon dropped out of the program. In hindsight, Daddy would have been far better served in a rehab facility than in that psychiatric ward.

That botched intervention is one of the many things I now believe could have had such different results if I had had more information and wherewithal; I would do it so differently now! I wish that at the time I'd said that the plan seemed wrong and suggested trying something else. I wish I could have started caring about what was best for Daddy right away, instead of it taking so long because I spent so much time dealing with the remnants he left behind.

And there I go again, drifting off into my regrets and even some remaining guilt I feel, even though I know, rationally, that those are not realistic thoughts—that I bear no responsibility for the fact that the intervention didn't work. Sometimes, when I catch myself slipping back into old patterns of guilt, I have to remind myself of things like that—I have to talk to myself like a counselor would, really; or like I would talk to someone who is currently in this situation, trying to help a loved one with an addiction. I'd say something like this: It's certainly understandable to have regrets about things we did or didn't do, and of course you must have been sad and disappointed that the intervention didn't work. But that does not mean you should be carrying any guilt on your shoulders. It's very common for the victim to want to help or fix the abuser. Again, on an emotional level, that is an entirely understandable reaction to terrible circumstances. But our more reasonable selves also have to remember that it is not our responsibility to help the addict, especially if he or she has also been our abuser; and moreover, it's actually not even very possible to fix things for an addicted person. Things like interventions sometimes do help and are certainly worth trying, so the person's family at least knows they've done all they could. The experts always say that the addict has to want to stop—that no one else can make him do it. But I know firsthand how difficult it can be to get out of those habits of trying to make things okay.

— — —

Serena left for college as I was going into my junior year of high school, and with her went any semblance of sanity at home. I lost my ally when Serena moved out, and I was left behind with a meaner Daddy and a weaker Karen. I felt terribly alone. Daddy's unpredictable, violent behavior seemed to take up even more space; the uncertainty about what might set him off loomed larger than before. More than ever, I lived in fear of him, and I imagine Karen did too.

Dinners had always been the worst part of the day. Throughout our childhoods, Daddy didn't spend much time with us, but dinner was the one time we had to interact with him for a prolonged period. After Serena left, I came to dread dinnertime even more than before. She'd been my ally, and the only other person on the planet who knew what it was like to live in my world.

I remember one particularly bad night when, as she usually did, Karen had made dinner. Her cooking was not great, but you couldn't blame her—when did she have time to cook? She had to work and support our family because Daddy was too busy drinking his life away in our den. On this occasion the rice wasn't cooked right, and Daddy got so mad he threw the platter toward Karen's head. Luckily it missed and crashed to the floor, scattering rice and broken bits of porcelain everywhere.

And it only got worse. One night, in one of Daddy's more irrational moments, he did something that made so little sense as it was happening that it feels hard to describe it coherently, but it happened exactly like this: Karen had been saying earlier that she might leave Daddy now that she had inherited some money of her own; that seemed to give her more strength and confidence. Armed with this newfound gumption, Karen began to shout back when Daddy yelled at her and hit her. They had just finished one of these shouting matches, and Karen wasn't speaking to Daddy, but we were still having dinner together, sitting at the kitchen table in dead silence. I was wearing a wrap shirt—the memory of it is indelible in my mind; it was a deep maroon color—and as I was putting a bite of chicken into my mouth, Daddy suddenly lunged across the table and ripped my shirt open. For a moment, the three of us just sat there, Karen and Daddy staring at my breasts at the kitchen table. Then I got over my shock enough to cover up. I remember feeling then that I was really not safe there anymore, that there was no longer even a semblance of rationality or normalcy left in that house.

I felt supremely alone in that moment. I knew no one would understand this story, not that I planned to go around talking about it, and I just felt like such a freak, stuck in this freak show life with these two miserable, selfish people and I knew I couldn't take much more.

Thank God, once again, for my friends. I called Sue, bawling hysterically, completely overwhelmed by then. Sue drove over to pick me up and take me to the sanctuary of her beautiful, loving home. I sat on her bed and told her what had happened. I cried and cried, and she cried and cried, and we talked for hours. Then she said, in the most loving, caring way possible, "Jess, this problem is getting too big for me. You have to talk to someone. I want you to talk with a counselor at school tomorrow."

Thus the road to safety and normalcy began for me, because my best friend was brave enough and strong enough to know that my alcoholic, inappropriate, abusive father was too big a problem for her to handle. Her amazing parents, with their love and guidance—which they often shared with me—had made Sue incredibly strong and smart. She literally changed my life by making me go see the school counselor.

When I sat down and talked with the counselor, she didn't seem as alarmed as I'd expected she would, which made me feel better. If she had acted all horrified, I don't think I would have shared as much with her, for fear of traumatizing her. I continued to see her regularly after that, and it really helped me. Of course, I don't remember many specifics about our conversations. I do remember her once saying, "You need to prepare yourself for the day when he's successful at killing himself." I didn't really know what she meant, but it stuck with me.

In those days mandatory reporting laws for child abuse weren't as understood or enforced. I begged my counselor not to say anything to anyone about what was going on in my home, for fear of being separated from my house, my cat, my friends; for fear of being put into foster care with strangers who might be even scarier than Daddy. And the counselor honored my request and kept my secret.

Later, Daddy actually tried to come up with an explanation for ripping his teenage daughter's shirt off at the dinner table: He said he didn't want Karen to feel alone, as the only one feeling mad at him; he thought she would feel better if I was mad at him too. You're probably rereading that last sentence and thinking, "Whaaat? I don't understand." Don't worry, neither do I.

— — —

During the summer before my senior year, Serena and I met someone we hadn't known existed: our half-sister. Daddy took us to meet Meredith at a restaurant, a seafood place called Phillips, though I can remember only a few other details of the lunch.

I remember being mortified that Daddy kept using racist slurs to refer to the waiters that day. I remember the overall oddness of the whole thing. I'd gone seventeen years thinking I had only one sister, and it was a shock to find out I had another one. Right away it was clear she was a lovely, kindhearted girl. And she looked so much like me, and even more like Daddy.

He hadn't known about Meredith either, for a long time. When Daddy first came to the States from Iran, he met the woman who would become Meredith's mom in the apartment complex they both lived in. She was deaf, and largely nonverbal, plus Daddy spoke very little English; I think their "relationship" was based on just one thing. Before long, he moved out of that apartment, and according to Daddy, she never told him she was pregnant, though I suspect he did actually know. Meredith was born about two years before Serena.

Daddy only really learned anything concrete about his first child when some lady from the bank kept calling our house, for weeks, and asking to speak with him—which seemed odd to me even then, because Daddy never handled any household duties. In almost twenty years, I don't think he ever once wrote a check. Karen signed his name on everything. Anyway, Daddy could tell I was suspicious about these phone calls, and he eventually told me that the girl who kept calling was actually our sister, pretending to work at the bank in the hope of getting him on the phone.

I know people are always telling stories about coincidences, but this has to be one of the grandest of all: After some bad luck, some dark times, and some wrong turns, Meredith ended up becoming a stripper . . . guess where? Yep—the very place that brought about my existence in this world: Dream Dolls. That's how she found Daddy; she was telling the owner of the club the story of her absent father, though she had no idea that he had worked there. Somehow the conversation led the owner to talk about Daddy, and they put it together that he was her father. And so Meredith tracked him down.

Meredith and Daddy had been corresponding for some

time before he allowed her to meet us. He was apparently trying to convince her to quit stripping and at first actually insisted she had to quit before she could meet us. But then he had a change of heart.

Talking to Meredith recently, I learned that on one of their first encounters, he picked her up, drunk of course, and drove her to meet Karen in the parking lot of our townhouse. I was probably inside, oblivious to the whole thing. Meredith said Daddy was speeding and so inebriated that he crashed into a parked truck. His side mirror shattered, and shards of glass flew in through his open window and cut his cheek.

The experience gave her a glimpse into our chaotic lives with Daddy. Plus, from that very first meeting, I was always very frank with her about his rages. I don't think she was too disappointed meeting him—she hadn't spent her childhood longing for him or anything, probably because she grew up with a very loving stepdad. I think she just wanted to meet Daddy out of curiosity about where she came from. And she would have liked to keep in touch with me and Serena, but Daddy didn't allow it, I imagine because she kept "dancing" at Dream Dolls.

I didn't see her again for years, until after Daddy died. Nowadays, Meredith and I talk quasi-regularly. She is a very good person, and happy too; we get along really well. She even came out to visit us with her two little boys last summer.

In the process of writing this book, especially the stuff about Daddy calling me a slut, I have finally summoned the courage to face something I had avoided for decades: Late in high school, when it was just me and Daddy and Karen in the house, Daddy made some attempts to sexually abuse me. Tearing my shirt open at dinner was just a precursor to worse incidents, where he crossed the line even further. Had I not been old enough to speak out and keep him away, it would have been devastating, and completely life changing.

I have only very recently started to share this aspect of my story when I speak to audiences. Even though it's been my life's work to talk about my abuse in order to help others, I left that part out for so long. It was just too painful, and I wasn't ready to disclose it to the whole world. I hope other victims who have heard me speak in the past will forgive me for keeping those memories locked in a dark little corner of my brain all those years.

Eventually, I began to feel like a hypocrite—urging people to share their stories of sexual abuse, when I was not willing to share mine. As I was writing this book, I realized I couldn't hide it anymore; I needed to talk about that part, to help heal current victims. I started slowly, telling only a few people I trust, and just saying it out loud those few times was healing. And I'm proud that, finally now, when it feels appropriate, I do talk about the attempted sexual abuse with certain groups I speak to, when I know that it might reach someone and help them. So far I've primarily told the teens and preteens I speak with. I know I'll eventually share it every time I tell my story.

His inappropriate behavior still haunts me. Those few incidents have left me with triggers that I deal with even now—every morning in the shower, for starters—and they carry with them an entirely different kind of pain than the physical and emotional abuse. The memories of those times are still nearly unbearable; they are embarrassing and humiliating and gross. They make me feel hollow and awful, and at the same time, enraged and disgusted. I'm sure the reason I still carry around such heavy feelings about those moments is that it took me so long to address them.

This is the part of the book that I am most scared for people in my family to read. That's a big reason many victims of sexual abuse, especially children, don't share—because very often people they love get upset with them and don't believe them.

It's amazing how hard I still find it to simply think about that part of my life, even though it was such a small window of time and the abuse didn't get as far as it might have. Nonetheless, I feel ashamed and disgusted by it. My own reluctance to disclose the sexual abuse explains a statistic I refer to every time I speak to an audience: one in four girls and one in six boys will be sexually abused before the age of eighteen, and yet only one in ten victims will tell about their abuse. Studies show that, just like it did for me, it takes many victims years to tell. As someone who is part of those statistics, I have incredible respect for victims of sexual abuse who speak out; it's been the hardest part for me. It breaks my heart to think about all the children who are suffering through such abuse in silence, because they're afraid their families will be ashamed of them, or worse yet, blame them.

— — —

After so many conversations with Karen about how she should leave Daddy—how we couldn't choose another Daddy, but she could choose another husband—she finally found the strength to leave. The seed had been planted when she got her inheritance; for her, with money came freedom. After seven years of marriage, and fifteen years of living together, their miserable relationship was finally over.

It was actually Daddy who moved out, during my senior year in high school, when Karen told him she wanted a divorce. As a minor, I had to choose to live with one of them, and as planned, I chose Karen. She and I stayed in our townhouse. Daddy moved back into Grandmother Parisa's house while they sorted out the divorce. He was confused about why I chose to live with Karen over him. So one day, I went over to my grandmother's house to explain.

I referenced this conversation earlier, but it had such an impact on my life, it warrants revisiting it in more detail. I could smell the cigarettes as I walked downstairs to his room.

I didn't quite realize then how sad he must have felt, how disappointed he must have been with his own life. One of Grandmother's lacy comforters was on the bed, and a few of his belongings were scattered around the room in an attempt to make it feel more like his own home.

Sad as it was, I felt like I had to say what I said to him then—and by that point, I wasn't very scared of him anymore. Once we were no longer living under his roof, his power seemed diminished. I felt more saddened than scared to say what I did. In the final analysis, I am glad I said it.

I told him I was sorry all this was going on. I told him I loved him, and always would, but that I didn't like him. The look on his face was of pure devastation. Now, as a mother, I can see how much pain those words must have caused him. He asked me why, with a bottomless longing and sadness. I began to recount some of the awful days. I told story after story. After each one, he cried and said he didn't remember any of it; and he said he was sorry.

At first it made me mad—these events had terrorized me and shaped me, and he didn't even remember them. But it wasn't surprising: He drank every day, practically around the clock because he was an insomniac. It makes sense that he didn't remember; he basically lived his life from blackout to blackout. And now, so many years later, it actually makes me feel a little better about it all because it helps explain the insanity and violence: He was sick. He was utterly, debilitatingly addicted to alcohol and drugs, and that's why he behaved as he did. It's no excuse for his behavior, but it is an explanation. And it made it easier for me to forgive him, later.

One crucial thing about that conversation: I didn't go into it with the expectation that he would be open to hearing what I said. I hoped for the best, of course, but I didn't count on it. This thinking was a way to protect myself in case it didn't have the outcome I wanted—which is partly what happened, when he told me he didn't remember any of the abuse. But his remorse and apologies were heartfelt, and that was significant to me. Maybe most importantly, I walked away from it knowing I had said everything I needed to say, for my own heart and my own healing.

I don't know how this was possible, but Daddy drank even more after he left. He also started breaking back into the townhouse to beat Karen up and drag her around the house by her hair. I was never home for any of these incidents, but I would come back later to the aftermath—the broken chain lock, the rug burns on Karen's face and arms. Once, the police showed up; I don't know who called them. Mostly, she would just cry and ask me what she should do. I was seventeen years old and had no idea what to tell her.

It didn't make things any easier that certain family members were furious at me for living with Karen instead of Daddy. They called me a traitor and said I was being disloyal to Daddy. I understand now that they were struggling to come to grips with the reality that their family member was an alcoholic and a wife and child abuser. But at the time, it really hurt, and it definitely added to my feelings of guilt and uncertainty to have relatives so angry at me.

I will say this for Daddy—unlike some of his relatives, he didn't bear a grudge against me for living with Karen. In fact, he really did right by me, during that time, by putting it in their divorce settlement that Karen had to support me financially until I got a college degree, and she had to pay for my college expenses too. He didn't ask for nearly as much as he could have for himself, because he wanted to make sure I had that. Only years later would I realize what a sacrifice that was; he was really struggling financially, and he could have asked for a lot of money for himself. Instead, he asked that his kids get a free ride to college. This was another reason it was possible to forgive Daddy—he did things like that. At the heart of him, buried so deep it emerged only occasionally, was a good, giving impulse.

— — —

I still relied heavily on my friends and stayed at their houses as much as possible. Sue was a constant, and during my senior year I also started spending lots of time at Michelle's. Her family was Persian, but that is where the similarities between our upbringings ended. Her father was a sweet, sensitive, happy man who laughed a lot; he even cried when he got emotional. Coincidentally, Michelle's grandfather had known my grandfather in Iran. I loved spending time at their house. Her dad helped give me hope that there were good men, and good fathers, in the world.

And I still pursued my holy grail, normalcy. I was working at the second animal hospital by then. I no longer worked with that boy Pat, but I did take him to my senior prom and laughed all evening with him and Sue. We all got hotel rooms that night, and I remember being so nervous that Pat might be "my first." It's funny, even with my memory lapses, I can still remember the pale peach bra and panty set I'd bought for that night—what does that say about the kind of person I am? Anyway, God gave me my period that day, so Pat and I just fooled around, and I was saved from making that decision way before I was ready.

Pat and I didn't last. Shortly after prom, his father died, and he kind of retreated into his family. We went to different schools and didn't see each other much, and we just drifted apart; there was no real drama. But I always loved my time with Pat; he was fun and sweet. I'm grateful that I had such a happy and safe first experience with romance.

— — —

One day when I was eighteen I was driving to Michelle's house, where I had driven literally hundreds of times, and I had one of my "weird day" episodes, as I so often did. That day I just despaired that I was lost yet again. I pulled over and cried. Mostly it was just extremely frustrating and unsettling, but sometimes it really scared me, feeling completely lost all the time. Eventually, as I always did, I shook it off and kept driving until something looked familiar and I could figure out how to get to Michelle's house. But when I got home later that day, I told Karen, again, that something was really wrong with me and asked that she please take me to a doctor so we could finally figure this out.

Out from under Daddy's thumb, Karen was feeling stronger and more independent. Without him there telling her I was fine, that my weird days were all in my head, she made some calls and got me an appointment with a neurologist. After I described my experiences, the doctor did an EEG and an MRI. And finally, when I was eighteen years old, I was diagnosed with temporal lobe epilepsy.

The doctor was kind of dumbfounded, having never heard of anyone having epilepsy for so many years and not getting treatment for it. She couldn't explain how I had learned to "fix" and stop the seizures—she had literally never heard of such a thing.

I can't express enough what an enormous relief it was to give this thing, these "weird days," a name and to know that I wasn't completely insane. And it makes me feel sort of proud of myself that all those years when Daddy was yelling at me to be strong, I was actually stronger than anyone knew, living with frequent seizures and dealing with them on my own. The epilepsy was ignored for so many years that it had become my normal.

And it continues to be to this day; I never went on the medication available for the disorder, and the doctor who diagnosed me said she couldn't blame me, seeing as how I'd lived so long without it. There are terrible side effects to the medication, including the possibility of having babies with birth defects. One constant in my crazy, chaotic life was that I knew with all my heart that one day I was going to make a new life for myself—my own good, happy, "normal" life as a mama. I wasn't going to risk that. And so today, I continue to live with epileptic seizures every day of my life.

Different people experience my type of seizures (temporal lobal seizures) differently. I don't lose awareness like some people do. For me, it's more that I get confused about my surroundings. I know I do this staring thing during seizures that is apparently common. And after a seizure, I sometimes have an inability to recall the events exactly as they occurred. But I am always aware of having seizures, both during and after.

Here's an example of how epilepsy affects my life today: I was recently driving to a meeting for child sexual abuse prevention in downtown Phoenix. While trying to find a parking lot, I had so many seizures that even with my GPS I couldn't figure out where the building was; I finally just left. When the seizures are that bad, and I am in an unfamiliar area, rather than try to "fix" it, I remove myself from the potentially dangerous situation. Those moments are so frustrating. On this day, I had to miss a meeting I had said I'd attend, and I couldn't tell anyone why because it wouldn't make sense. It's especially hard when I get lost on my way to a meeting that is somewhere I've been countless times.

Certain things can trigger my seizures—flickering lights, like when there is a light on a ceiling fan, or sunlight flickering through leaves (which makes me a little bit sad, because looking at trees brings me such a great sense of peace—but I have to be careful about it!). I've learned that epilepsy is different for everyone. One of my symptoms is that I always think I smell cigarettes; I didn't know that was because of my epilepsy until a good friend who is a neurosurgeon told me. Scientists also say that stress can bring on seizures.

I've kept my epilepsy a secret for a very long time. I just recently started telling people about it, but now that I am I want to take this opportunity to apologize to all the people whose names I regularly forget, to everyone who has been in the car with me when I've gone the wrong way, and to those who have waited for me when I've been late for a meeting. Please know that my terrible memory and sense of direction are results of my epilepsy!

In the Adverse Childhood Experience (ACES) study I talked about earlier, one of the conclusions was that extreme neglect—to the point of not taking your child to the doctor in the face of alarming symptoms—is a form of child abuse. When I think about all those years during my childhood when I was frequently struck by seizures—by a sudden and complete disorientation and sense of being lost in the world—and had no idea why it was happening and no one to help me, it seems almost like a metaphor for all the other ways I felt disoriented and adrift and scared because of my father's abuse. Except that it wasn't a metaphor; it was a very real and scary disorder that I struggled with alone for many years. And then I think about the fact that I figured out how to manage it all on my own; I admit, I feel pretty proud of myself for that! I also feel very encouraged by it, because if I did that, then all the children I'm trying to help through my work surely also have inner reserves of strength to see them through their own challenges.

Daddy felt terrible when I told him about the diagnosis. He couldn't believe I'd been having seizures all those years, and he carried a lot of guilt about it afterward. He apologized for not taking me to the doctor for it when I was little. And that really meant something to me.

— — —

My graduation from high school was memorable, Daddy made sure of that. Like everyone else, I'd bought a white dress and shoes to match. I remember sitting in the rows of metal folding chairs in the auditorium, paying very little attention as the principal gave a speech about something to do with international affairs, probably the Persian Gulf War, which was happening at the time. I was sitting next to my friend Zara, whose last name was nearly identical to mine—they were different by just two letters, though she was Malaysian, not Persian.

Daddy began shouting loudly and incoherently from the stands, every other word or so a swear word. Suddenly my pristine white dress and shoes meant zero; instead of feeling pride and excitement at this big milestone, I was so humiliated I might as well have been sitting there naked. Zara knew who was doing the heckling, but thank God other people didn't catch on.

In the envelope with my high school diploma was my final report card. By this point, Karen and Daddy never remembered to ask about my grades, so I knew neither of them would care. I think I threw it immediately into the trash. Our class ranking was also there—I was about second to last. I didn't really mind. When your dad's periodically trying to kill you, your sister, your stepmom, or himself, things like class ranking don't seem all that relevant!

A bunch of us went to Zara's boyfriend's house after graduation. There I met a boy who was a much-needed diversion, and nice to look at to boot. He also smelled good; later, when he was back at college and we exchanged some letters, they always smelled like him. Our letter writing was sweet and romantic and something that will probably never happen to my daughter, because boys just don't do that kind of stuff anymore; almost no one, male or female, writes and mails actual letters these days. Nothing ever came of me and that kindhearted boy; we never really had a beginning or an end, just that little blush of a romance. Nonetheless, his presence that night of my graduation, and his normalcy, were a gift. He probably didn't know what a lovely glow he cast on that otherwise awful night.

CHAPTER 7

The period after graduation got a little chaotic; it's kind of blurry in my memory. I had planned to go to college and room with Sue. We both got into Lynchburg college, a lovely college that cared more about how much money you could pay in tuition than your GPA, which is how I got accepted. But I had gotten so caught up in the mess of my life that I'd become something of a recluse. For her part, Sue was just being a normal teenager, doing the things normal teenagers do, including partying sometimes, and I didn't like that. The toll alcohol abuse had taken on my life simply kept me from being able to have a normal view of drinking. I couldn't watch as she conducted what was, in reality, just a normal teenage girl's life in the summer before college. The stress and strain of my life, and my disdain for drinking alcohol, drove a wedge between me and my best friend and lifeline. We started to drift apart. And though we were going to the same college, we decided not to room together. Thank goodness our friendship survived that short period when we were out of step with each other.

So instead of heading off to college in my best friend's red Honda Civic—I'd imagined us diving into a new life adventure together—Karen drove me to school in Lynchburg, Virginia, with my navy blue trunk full of my most treasured possessions. We drove the windy roads in virtual silence. It was strange, but I felt like I was really going to miss Karen.

Lynchburg College was postcard pretty, with its beautiful old brick buildings, lush green grass, and big gorgeous trees.

The campus was tiny; I could see the whole thing from my dorm room window, which overlooked the quadrangle. In the fall, the leaves turned those unreal hues of red and yellow that they do in Virginia.

However, I took very little pleasure in being there. I probably wasn't ready for college anyway, but what really ruined it for me was that Daddy and Karen started calling all the time to tell me their woes. Daddy would say he was terribly lonely and wanted to die; he told me he was going to kill himself, over and over and over. Karen would call me crying, also saying how alone she felt or to tell me about another break-in by Daddy. Each of them claimed I was the only person they could talk to. They were relentlessly self-involved, and at the time I did not have it in me to figure out how to live my own life, for myself. Even though I was living away from home for the first time, I felt as trapped by them as ever, bogged down by guilt about how I'd left them both in their great time of need.

But there were other reasons college life didn't agree with me—like the drinking. At pretty much every college, especially the small ones in small towns where there's little to do, everyone drank alcohol all the time and did pretty much nothing else. For my part, I began straying occasionally from my strict anti-drinking stance, and I vacillated between drinking so much I couldn't remember why I was sad and never wanting to see an alcoholic beverage again in my life.

Alcohol is such a hot spot when you're the child of an alcoholic. For me, drinking much at all just feels wrong, and it's been like that my entire adult life. I have never had a sip of alcohol in front of my kids, and I rarely drink in public. I usually opt to stay in control and not drink. For many years I actually didn't drink at all, not one sip, even on my wedding day. I just don't like that feeling of not being in control; it feels unsafe to me. That's been my response to being the product of people who couldn't say no to overindulgence. I worry I'll be like them if I indulge myself. Since starting my work in child abuse prevention, I've learned that many children who grow up in homes like mine take the opposite course and follow exactly in their parents' footsteps. I don't know why some of us stay away from alcohol when others develop their own addictions, but I feel lucky.

Anyway, I can only remember a couple of college parties that felt like what college life should feel like—a roomful of animated faces, that happy hum of voices, cute guys checking out cute girls, people dancing and doing Jell-O shots. And I had a couple of normal flirtations with cute, sweet boys.

One good thing about college was my kindhearted roommate. She was also gorgeous—that kind of beautiful-no-matter-what gorgeous. The boys went nuts for her, and I did too—her heart was even lovelier than her face. She was beautiful, sweet, popular— everyone loved her—and she was so kind to me. She knew I was struggling. I don't remember how much I shared with her, but she never made me feel bad for being so down and she always tried to get me to partake in the normal college fun she was having. But my heart just wasn't in it. She and I lived pretty separate lives, despite sharing about 200 square feet of living space. I could feel there was sadness in her life too; she just didn't let it drag her down like I did during that period.

I made another friend at college who was my salvation while I was there. She made me laugh until I cried. She, too, had suffered a lot in her life, and she showed me that you can have life after tragedy. I hold her in my heart always, even though I never get to talk to her anymore. So even there in Lynchburg, where I felt trapped in a living hell, God gave me friends. He has always, always given me excess in the friend department, to make up for my family, I guess. I relish in the joys all my friendships have always brought me.

But the majority of my time at Lynchburg, I was in turmoil,

thanks to the endless calls from home. I failed every class, and left after just one semester.

— — —

Discouraged and fairly depressed, I moved back in with Karen and started at a community college in Springfield. I also worked at the animal clinic with the two vets who started their own place; that was a bright spot in my life. Karen was in her new house by then. After the divorce was finalized, she'd moved out of the townhouse we shared with Daddy and bought a huge house—much bigger than she and Serena and I needed. But eventually, Karen proved almost as hard to live with as the chaos I was trying to escape.

Karen started getting weirder and weirder during that time. She starting drinking and smoking pot openly, and her psychiatrist was also giving her prescription meds. The weirdest thing was that she started dating her stepbrother, an "artist" who I always believed was only in it to get some of Karen's newfound bucks—she "loaned" him thousands of dollars to help him jump-start his career. I didn't like having him around the house. On one occasion, I even walked in on them when they were "hot and heavy" in the middle of the family room.

Things came to a head one day when Serena was home visiting. It was a weekend morning, and I was trying to sleep in when all of a sudden Serena burst into my room, shouting, "Wake up, Jessica; wake up! You need to come downstairs right now!" She grabbed my hand and pulled me downstairs. Karen's stepbrother/boyfriend was there, and apparently he had raised his hand to hit my sister. There was a huge confrontation, lots of yelling, and the disgusting stepbrother raised his hand to hit Serena again, telling us to stop taking out our anger at Daddy on him.

Right then and there, I told Karen to choose between him—I think the phrase I used was "this loser"—and us, the girls she called her daughters. Karen said nothing, her chin quivering as she looked straight down at the ground. And so the decision was made.

— — —

Daddy was so happy when we decided to move out of Karen's house that the next day he went with me to look for my own apartment. It was one of the few normal things we ever did together. Not that he was generally behaving any better. We stopped at the grocery store that day, and as we walked out, a car drove by and didn't stop to let us cross the street. Daddy used his steel-toed boot to kick in the passenger door. They were smart or lucky enough not to turn around and confront him.

I moved into my own apartment, back in our old neighborhood, off Carrleigh Parkway. That was when I got my own first cat who was really just mine. I bought her from a breeder; she was a blue point Himalayan named Princess. And I was back to working at the animal hospital with my same great boss from before. He bought me a pumpkin for my first Halloween on my own and then a tiny Christmas tree. He wanted to make sure that I still celebrated the holidays properly even though I was living alone. I was so grateful that he always looked out for me like that, and I loved working for him.

For some reason I can't remember, though, I left to work at Happy Harry's Pizza—as a hostess, because Daddy said I was never allowed to be a waitress. "No daughter of mine will wait on people! People should be waiting on you!" But soon I disobeyed him and switched from hosting to serving; he never found out about that. Waiting tables was challenging in some ways. I hated how picky people were about their food. And my memory issues made it hard; I must have gone through twenty notepads a night taking orders because I literally wrote down every single thing the customers said. I did well at it, though, and I made great money. I could hold six beer "schooners," huge glasses like fishbowls on stems, which always impressed my tables—so that once they were full of a schooner of beer, they usually gave me great tips!

I actually think everyone should wait tables when they're young. I've already told my monkeys they will wait tables, just for a little while, to gain life experience. Plus, it makes you so much more patient at restaurants because you know how hard the work is.

I loved working at Happy Harry's. I loved the camaraderie among the staff. It was especially fun after closing time, while we all cleaned our stations. We played loud music and hung out, and there was always a lot of laughter. I became good friends with the other hostess. And I also met my first real boyfriend.

When I first met Mark, I didn't think about him romantically because he wasn't my type physically, with his brown hair and brown eyes; I am most attracted to blond-haired, blue-eyed, all-American boys. But Mark was hilariously funny; he made me laugh until I cried. After working with him for a while, I started to fall for him. We used to make out like crazy in the restaurant's freezer. I'm sure that broke about a million health codes!

I was fortunate that I loved all my jobs. Work was so important for me at that age. It helped give me sense of independence and of my own identity and worth. I'm sure I enjoyed work partly because I didn't rely on it as my sole source of income.

Shortly after I moved into my first place alone, when I was nineteen, Daddy moved to Florida. That had been his plan for some years. He had a number of relatives there, including a cousin he really liked and his youngest brother, whom we almost never saw (he had been the last of the siblings to move to America from Iran). One of his sisters lived there for a while, too. We vacationed there a couple of times when I was a kid. I think he moved there because he was just looking for the happiness that always seemed to elude him.

Originally, we were all supposed to move to Florida. Had Karen not fallen into her money and finally summoned the courage to leave, the three of us would have moved there, and Serena would have come for school holidays. I was very relieved when it didn't happen; I'd been dreading being stuck with Daddy and Karen alone in a place where I knew no one.

So Daddy went to live on his own in a little townhouse in Clearwater, Florida. And something kind of remarkable happened: Maybe it was because he was out of his comfort zone and his routine, but for the first time, he really tried to stop drinking and to change his ways. He started taking meds that were supposed to make his body reject alcohol. In the end, the medications didn't work, but at least he'd become conscious of his drinking problem and truly tried to do something about it. During that period when Daddy tried to get sober, he remembered my birthday and always sent me a card and a gift. That was a big deal for me.

He also started dating someone, which surprised me—and initially I was a little bit worried that he would beat her up like he had Karen, but that didn't ever happen as far as I know. Francine a friend of Daddy's cousin's wife; he met her through them and somehow they became a couple. She was originally from far away, too—from Poland, and she had a thick accent. Maybe they connected in part because they both felt like outsiders. Anyway, they seemed fairly happy together.

I have a few memories from the one time I visited him in Florida, with my cousin Saeed. It was actually a very pleasant visit. For once, his home felt pretty peaceful. There was no yelling when I was there, and he was very smiley. Daddy had fixed up the guest room and spare bathroom for me; that meant a lot. He had even bought little hand towels with the letter "J" initialed on them, just for me. They were one of the first things he showed me when I got there; he was super proud of them. My old dog Lucky, a fluffy little cream-colored Pomeranian, had gone to Florida with Daddy, and it was fun to see him.

Francine had moved in by then, and I remember sitting down to eat with them at their kitchen table. It was so unlike any meal I'd ever had with Daddy. He seemed happy. It was so nice to have that time with him and to be able to hold in my heart a few good memories of him.

By this point in my life, I had started to feel so sad and sorry for Daddy. He was very fragile emotionally, constantly talking about ending his life. It made it easier to forgive him for everything. It was clear to me by now that he wasn't the strong man he'd tried to act like his whole life. I saw that he was actually very weak and almost incapable of being a functioning member of society. There I was in college, working, becoming a productive adult, while he hadn't held a job for well over ten years. His problems and his sadness felt so dark and deep, like they went way back into the misty past when he hadn't become a military pilot in Iran, his promise extinguished before it was even really lit. It felt so strange, like I was the adult now, worrying about him. I was always trying to think of work he could do, but he shot down every idea; he said he couldn't do or be anything in life. On top of that, he told me that he never felt like he belonged anywhere, or with anyone. And I didn't know how to help him.

— — —

I've thought a lot about how much I missed out on by not having two functioning, contented parents. Lately I realized that, beyond never having role models for the big stuff—like how to be a good person and how to create a happy home—I also grew up with no idea of how to behave on a very basic, day-to-day level out in the world. Instead, I watched Daddy slamming through life and Karen sort of fumbling through it, neither of them with any sense of how to interact with other people in public. Trips to the grocery store were always a bit embarrassing because Karen seemed to be the most socially awkward person alive, especially with men. Or if I was with Daddy, he would more than likely badger the checkout person and the bagger, often throwing slurs at them. On a good day, he would merely stare them down with his evil "go ahead and try to say something to me" glare.

I was recently out with my husband and my two beautiful children, and I was watching my husband chat with the wife of one of his dear friends. At that moment, I thought how I never—not once during my entire childhood—saw Daddy talk to a woman who wasn't family or saw Karen talk to any men outside of the family, aside from the reverend at our church. I'm so grateful that my children get to see first-hand how to interact with other people, because not knowing that it was okay for men and women to interact with members of the opposite sex outside of the family caused me to feel pretty insane during my first foray into dating.

Poor Mark Winters. Here was this totally normal, sociable guy who had some close, long-standing friends who happened to be girls. I simply couldn't deal with that; I felt so threatened by those girls and desperately jealous of their friendships with Mark. I argued with the poor guy about it on a regular basis, and it drove him up the wall. I met Mark too soon after being immersed in the madness of my household, and I wasn't nearly ready for a relationship.

Nonetheless, we kept at it for a couple of years, and it was an important, and often happy, experience for me. For instance, he was the first boy I told about my painful family life. It happened by accident, actually; usually Mark and I just laughed and had fun. His sense of humor and his playfulness were a huge diversion from the intense sadness and pressure of my life up until then. But one night we were watching a movie in which the main character, who was an adult, went home to see her father and he ended up beating her savagely. She kept trying to get up off the ground and he just kept kicking her. It flooded me with memories and I started to cry hysterically. Mark had no idea what was going on, or what to do. He turned the movie off and we went and lay on the bed. He hugged me while I told him about my childhood, and he promised that he would never let anyone hurt me again. I'll never forget how amazing that felt. Another great aspect of our relationship was being Mark's mom and sister; they were so sweet and loving, and they gave me another glimpse of the kind of family I wanted one day.

About a year and a half into our relationship, Mark decided to move to Arizona to become a professional golfer. That sounded exciting, and I was more than ready to get far away from the place where I'd spent my childhood, so I decided to go with him. He went ahead of me, and I stayed in Springfield for a few months while I planned my new life out West. For starters, I applied to Arizona State University, in those days a long process of mailing paperwork back and forth and making many telephone calls. Once I got accepted, I found myself an apartment, which entailed getting a catalog of rental apartments in the mail and calling every place that looked nice to see how close it was to the school. Things were really different before the Internet!

The plan was I'd stay in Virginia through mid-July so that I could spend one last summer selling fireworks, to make some cash. After that, I would head off to begin my Arizona adventure.

Then something terrible happened: Mark's best friend's dad committed suicide, and it hit Mark hard. I remember standing at the funeral of this man, a hugely celebrated Vietnam vet, in Arlington National Cemetery and not understanding how someone who had made it through so much had decided, nearly twenty years after surviving that horrible war, to end his life. Along with the pain he felt for Kevin and his family, Mark started re-evaluating his own life, as often happens when death hits close to home. He thought about how short life is, and how young he was, and whether, at that stage, he really wanted a serious relationship with an uber-needy girlfriend.

The upshot was a knife inserted into my heart, and twisted around for good measure. He wasn't mean about it, but still, I was 100 percent certain I wouldn't survive the heartbreak. After he called to say he didn't think we should be together anymore, I lay on the floor of my bedroom, next to my white iron bed with the purple flowered Laura Ashley comforter, telling my friend Michelle I would never recover and that there was just no way I would ever love anyone else, for the rest of my days.

On top of my broken heart, I had already given my landlord in Springfield notice and paid a deposit on a little apartment in Tempe, Arizona, which I was still at that point pronouncing incorrectly, as half the country does. (I was saying "Temp"; the correct pronunciation is "Temp-pee.") And I was still desperate to get out of Springfield. Thank God that Mark still cared enough to drive back to Virginia to get me, then make the cross-country trek with me to get me—and my cat Princess, of course—settled into my new apartment in the desert.

In retrospect, I don't blame Mark one bit for ending things. I was such a hot mess at the time, and he was such a happy-go-lucky, fun spirit. I would have squashed some of that exuberance out of him, especially since my life didn't get a lot easier for some time after that.

I'm still grateful to him for getting me to Arizona. I would never have come here had it not been for him. I'm also grateful for the love he gave me; I had never known anything like it before. It was just as first love should be: full of happiness and laughter, a little heartache, and a lot of lessons. I had a huge learning curve ahead of me when it came to relationships, and Mark Winters, with his sweetness and high energy, helped me up and over it. Whenever I think of him, it is always with a smile.

So there I was, finally far from home, out in the big world—and the first couple months were super lonely. Mostly, of course, it was because I was still heartbroken, but I found other things to make me blue as well. I really wondered if moving had been the wrong decision.

For one thing, the Arizona landscape was so different from Virginia, and I didn't like it at first. I desperately missed my trees and pretty green lawns. I found it very strange that many of the front yards in Arizona were covered in rocks. But that loss of a beloved landscape was nothing compared to the loss of the friends I'd left behind in Virginia. I was totally alone except for my ex-boyfriend, a few streets away. At first, I didn't even have a television to distract me! My TV was being shipped from Virginia, and this was before the days when I'd just hop over to Target and buy a new one.

It seemed to come slowly at the time, but I did eventually begin to feel better. I started school. Although I didn't have any friends yet, I had Princess. My broken heart healed a little bit. I even went on a couple of dates. Most gratifyingly, I began to get serious about entering a state-level pageant. Gradually, I felt ready to start my life.

CHAPTER 8

And then, four months after I moved to Arizona, on my twenty-first birthday, I met Dave Nicely.

I was running late for school—a pretty regular occurrence, as you will by now not be surprised to hear—and when I turned into the vast parking lot I saw, out of the corner of my eye, a little blue car pulling in nearby. I've always been big on trusting my instincts; I suppose it's an important trait when you grow up in a hostile home where you have to constantly be on the alert. I got out of the car and, still just looking kind of sidelong, I saw a tall, blond guy emerge from the blue car. We started walking in the same direction, and then more or less side by side, keeping the same stride. And though I hadn't yet seen his face because I hadn't looked at him head-on, I got this overwhelming feeling that I needed to talk to this person.

So I turned to this tall blond man who was now walking right next to me and I said just that: "I really felt like I needed to talk to you." I couldn't help but notice then that, lucky for me, the tall blond was extremely handsome: strong jaw line, lovely bone structure. He said, "Okay . . ." in a bit of a questioning tone, probably wondering if I was totally nuts. And we just started talking, and continued to for some time because Arizona State is so big. We finally arrived at my building, Language and Lit, and said good-bye. I was about to head inside when he came racing back and said, "I swear I never do this, but I'd really like to see you again," and asked for my number. I told him that I literally never gave my number to strangers—and then proceeded to share my number with this stranger whom I'd just met, because of the feeling I got that I was meant to talk with him.

That night, Mark Winters took me out to dinner, because it was my birthday and he knew I didn't know anyone in the area. I proceeded to tell him all about Dave and how I'd gotten that feeling; I said that I thought he might be the one. I was super excited, and Mark was genuinely happy for me. He was his usually jolly self as we ate a yummy dinner.

Dave and I went on our first date the next day. He took me to Red Lobster and I'll never forget how we sat under this little sign that said "Romance Under the Sea." He was blond and hazel-eyed and sweet; he'd played baseball very seriously, earlier in college—he'd even been looked at by some major league teams—but he didn't play any longer. Mostly, I was struck by how happy he seemed. It became clear very early on that Dave and I had lived vastly different lives. His parents, still happily married, had been high school sweethearts. With them and his older brother, he had led a terrifically happy, simple, and, yes, normal life. They played board games together, for goodness sake! I was instantly drawn to Dave and this family he was telling me about.

Dave was still living at home with his parents, and so on that first date, after dinner and a movie (*Shawshank Redemption* was our first movie), we went to his house. While his parents slept, Dave and I sat on their couch watching another movie and then talking late into the night.

I quickly became immersed in Dave's life. His family welcomed me with love and happiness. They had lots of dinners together, and lots of game nights. His parents played on a softball team and we'd go watch their games. Dave and his brother and their dad all played on a softball team together, too. They laughed a lot. I hadn't counted on this part, but becoming a part of this family that was so unlike mine actually took some getting used to. Dave's father is pretty much the kind of daddy I'd always dreamed of having—patient, happy, loving. He made me feel part of the Nicely family instantly. Dave's brother had a lovely wife and a beautiful baby boy, just three months old when I came into Dave's life. There was so much love and so much normalcy; it was wonderful. I got to spend my first Thanksgiving and Christmas in Arizona with Dave's beautiful family.

For the next couple of years, I settled deeply into life in Arizona. I continued to attend school, and I got a job at an animal clinic. I reveled in my relationship and the newfound family it had brought me. And I prepped a ton for the Miss Arizona pageant. For starters, I watched videos of previous pageants religiously, studying the winners intensely—the way they walked down the stage, their final answers during their interviews, their facial expressions as they listened to the host ask questions. I practiced my walk and interview. I assembled a folder of helpful tools, studied my magazines, taught myself how to apply makeup.

I also thought long and hard about what social issues I wanted to focus on, both as a contestant and, if I was lucky enough to win, during the year when I would "reign" as Miss Arizona. When I was researching past competitions, the title holders I most admired had given back to their communities in some way. It was so inspiring—I saw that if I won, I could use my painful childhood to help others. How fantastic would that be, if I could turn the worst parts of my life into opportunities to ease other people's suffering.

A couple of years in, my no-longer-so-new life in Arizona was full, exciting, and, finally, pretty normal.

— — —

My grandmother Elizabeth's health started to decline when I moved to Arizona. Several months after Dave and I started dating, I took him to Vermont so he could meet her. She was already in the hospital by then; it was the last place I saw her alive. Even then, so frail and tiny from her illness, hooked up to a breathing apparatus in a roomful of people— still her eyes would lock for a moment with grandfather's, and their love filled up the whole space.

Five months after that visit, Grandmother Elizabeth died. Serena and I went to the funeral in Vermont. I felt bereft at her death. And just as difficult was seeing my devastated grandfather, alone now. For the last few months of her life, when they'd known she was not going to make it, they'd moved a hospital bed into their family room. Grandfather got one, too, so he could sleep right next to her. She was his best friend, his constant companion. I was sure he wouldn't be able to bear life without her and would follow her soon.

I had two amazing, unexplainable experiences when I was in Vermont for the funeral. The first was that I found Grandmother's last, unfinished letter to me, in a kitchen drawer. I keep this letter in my Bible with the other one. Although she had started to write it before she was hospitalized, already by that point she could hardly write; she was too weak. Her handwriting, so familiar and beloved, had deteriorated. It was like a gift, this last letter waiting for me in the drawer.

She'd written it in response to a letter I had sent them saying how much it meant to me to have them in my life and how their love for each other gave me faith that love between a husband and wife was very possible. I'd thanked them for loving me and for being such a beautiful example for me. This was her reply, as much as she could muster the strength for:

Dear sweetest Jessie,

What a precious letter, you make us feel that our lives have really counted. And passing our love, hopes and dreams on to you is the greatest gift we could ever hope for. Love for your husband and family is the most precious, and it's free from God.

And then the letter stops; she must not have had the strength to continue. It's not lost on me that the last word my grandmother wrote to me was His name.

Then there was a magical moment right after the funeral. Everyone else had gone, but Serena and I stayed sitting at her gravesite for a bit longer. Serena said a girl had once told her that at her own grandmother's funeral, a butterfly had landed on her grave marker, and the girl had felt so comforted by it. I said I wished that would happen to us. And at that moment, a little yellow butterfly came and sat on my finger. Serena and I looked at each other in total disbelief, and I knew with all my heart that Grandmother had made it happen.

That's why I love butterflies so much—it's why I wanted a butterfly as the logo for Winged Hope. To this day, whenever I see a butterfly—which is all the time—I feel Grandmother Elizabeth near me.

Grandfather loved hearing about these amazing experiences, and he told me about one of his own: That morning before her funeral, he noticed a book out of place on a shelf. He pulled it out and saw that a passage was marked—and it was about a wife's love for her husband.

It was truly such a miraculous trip, and it felt very peaceful to me. Grandmother still felt so present, even though she was gone; that feeling made it much easier for me to handle her passing. But I worried about Grandfather and what he would do with himself now that his wife was gone.

But Grandfather not only survived her death, he actually lived years and years beyond her. He died peacefully in 2006. He was still alive when email became a regular form of communication, and it felt very special to be able to send emails back and forth with him, especially because he wasn't as much of a talker as my grandmother had been. I still have some of his emails.

And once again, when Grandfather died, I had an incredible

experience. My uncle—Patty's brother—was going through Grandfather's belongings, cleaning out the house, and he came across a letter Grandfather had written to me. I had written him months before, asking him for details about his and Grandmother's courtship. Grandmother had told me all about it, but I wanted it documented. And amazingly, God ensured that yet again, I had another letter waiting for me when I was back in Vermont for Grandfather's funeral. I still have that wonderful letter, the last one he ever wrote. I still miss him and my grandmother very much.

— — —

I had by now been preparing for pageants for years. I'd continued watching and studying the tapes. I had familiarized myself with every current event imaginable and had learned about myself inside and out, so I could easily express my thoughts and opinions on every relevant subject; I was ready to answer any question. I had also been working out like a fiend and had the body I thought I needed to win. I was ready; this was my year, 1996. I was twenty-two. I resolved to go in there with everything I had, even though I wasn't really sure where or what "there" was, having never done it before.

I looked through the yellow pages and called information. Eventually I located the national number for Miss USA, and from them I got the state director's contact information. I called her to ask about the process of applying, and she sent me an application, which I competed and submitted with my photo. And that was that—I was officially a contestant in the Miss Arizona USA pageant. I felt prepared, and I planned to win.

Daddy wanted to come watch me compete; it was the one time he visited me in Arizona. I was really surprised he wanted to come and somewhat nervous for his arrival; anyone who's been abused will know what I mean when I say that the very presence of the abuser can shake your world up. But I was also very touched that he was coming.

When he showed up, though, I saw that he was drinking again. For much of the visit, he was moody and mean, though as I'd gotten older, he really tried hard to curb his temper. In any case, I put on my happy face, determined not to let him get me down, and proceeded to compete.

I picked my dress off the rack at Neiman Marcus, which is something most pageant girls don't do. It was modest and ivory-colored, with a layer of lace over it. For the swimsuit part, I chose a black one-piece. I brought a Cindy Crawford Revlon ad to the pageant to remind myself how I wanted to apply my eye makeup. Dave and his parents and some of my friends were there cheering me on. My cousin Saeed was there, and two of my aunts. For the three days of competition, I stayed in the hotel in Phoenix where the pageant was held. It was thrilling to be living out my dream.

The pageant itself was surreal, and went by very quickly. Being backstage was exciting and a little bit overwhelming. Another contestant, an incredibly sweet girl, really helped me with all the little details of competition that I knew nothing about back then—for instance, that you should use "butt glue" so your bathing suit doesn't ride up. She also helped me perfect my stance. Right before I was supposed to go onstage for each event, I got terribly nervous. I had the biggest butterflies in my stomach; I'm not really someone who throws up, but if I was, I definitely would have in those moments. Thank God for that girl—right before I went out onstage, every time, she held my hands and prayed with me, and it calmed me. The time onstage went so fast, I barely had a chance to even register what was happening.

After the first round of competition, during a short intermission, Daddy said to me, "You have a 50/50 shot, but I think the black girl is gonna win." He was talking about the girl who had prayed with me. I thought so, too. She had competed before so she really knew what she was doing, and she was very beautiful and kindhearted.

I realized some time later that Daddy's drunken presence may have actually helped me win. During the interview, when I was asked about the biggest problem facing our nation and how I would solve it, I don't think I could have been any more passionate in my answer that drugs and alcohol are our nation's toughest battle because they are the precursor to so many other crimes—child abuse, rape, gun violence, gang violence, drunk driving, and the list goes on and on. With Daddy there, drunk, the dreadful addiction that had plagued my life was fresh in my heart, and it lent even greater conviction to my answer.

The rest of the pageant is all a bit of a blur. I was, of course, dazzled when I won. And surprised: I'd really expected that lovely girl to win. She ended up being the first runner-up. She was just extraordinarily giving and caring. We still talk sometimes. She really did help me win; I owe her a great debt for her generosity that night.

A side note: I actually found that most of the contestants were kind. In my later experience competing and then coaching girls in the pageant world, I saw that people are generally as nice to you as you are to them. Sure, there are sometimes divas or otherwise bad seeds, but that is the exception not the norm—though, of course, they stand out and give the rest of us a bad name.

Everyone was excited for me for winning, including Daddy, and I felt doubly lucky—to have won and to have so many people who loved me. We all celebrated at the Arizona Biltmore, and Dave and I got a room so I could continue celebrating the big win with my friends; it made the night feel even more special. Also, I didn't want to go back to Daddy and the apartment. I was really uncomfortable sleeping in my tiny one-bedroom apartment with Daddy drunk on the couch, continuing to drink all night long and into the next morning.

— — —

There are always certain friends who like to share with strangers that I was Miss Arizona. After the initial once-over that usually follows, I can always tell right away which ones are viewing me differently; there's an expression they get on their face, like, "Well, doesn't she just think she's the @!#%!" But that actually couldn't be further from the truth—I am like almost every pageant girl I've ever known, riddled with insecurities. Mine are about my appearance. I always think I'm not pretty enough or skinny enough, that my hair is too thin, my thighs are too big, my skin is really starting to look "old," and—the one that has been with me for as long as I can remember—my nose is way, way, way too big.

I'm quite certain any first-year psych major would say that this insecurity started with Daddy's pet name for me, "Meatball Nose," which is pretty self-explanatory: It looked like there was a giant meatball stuck to the end of my giant nose! How's that for a confidence booster? When he wasn't ignoring me or telling me I was a slut, I was meatball nose. How did I end up with friends? How did I walk away from that house with any confidence whatsoever? When I tell my story in public, people ask me that all the time, and I'm never 100 percent sure of the answer, except faith in God and hope; I held on to a constant hope and faith that my life was going to get better, that it would become all I wanted it to be, despite my meatball nose and other challenges. God, faith, and my friends all conspired to keep me sane.

— — —

The day after my win, Daddy said he wanted to go do something—he didn't use these words, but I knew he meant he wanted to go sightseeing or do something fun. He liked Arizona and commented many times on its resemblance to Iran, which seemed to make him happy. As far as I could tell, he didn't have anything to drink before we headed out to the

Phoenix Zoo, one of my favorite places.

I remember that day so vividly. Daddy and I had hardly ever done anything just the two of us; I had only a handful of memories of such times. He hadn't come to my soccer games when I was growing up; he hadn't dropped me off or picked me up from school. Pretty much the only alone time I had with him during my childhood was spent trapped in our house with him drunk.

Daddy looked for a shirt with an image of a wolf at the zoo gift shop, but he couldn't find the perfect one so he asked me to find one later and send it to him. And he did something surprising that day at the zoo. Daddy—who seemed to love to call me slut or meatball nose, who thought I had a 50/50 shot of winning the pageant, who hated everyone and spoke to almost no one unless he was shouting at them—that same man turned to a trolley full of people and called out, "This is my daughter; she is Miss Arizona!" Everyone on the trolley started clapping, and Daddy looked so proud. It's nice to have that memory, of a proud Daddy.

I can't help but think of what-ifs: What if Daddy had tried harder more of the time? What if he had made an effort for more trips like the one to the zoo? Maybe he would have seen how nice life can be when you're present in the moment, when you're sober, and when you're being the kind of dad your children need.

— — —

I spent 1997 as Miss Arizona and continued through the pageant circuit, which meant I participated in the Miss USA pageant. Daddy came to that one too—and so did Karen! I made sure they never crossed paths. She was still afraid of him, and pretty much hated him, so she stayed far away.

In any case, I knew I wanted to use my newfound spot in the public eye to spread awareness about child abuse and domestic violence. I got in touch with the National Committee to Prevent Child Abuse and then with the Arizona chapter of what is now known as Prevent Child Abuse America. Soon I was traveling the state as the organization's spokesperson.

But before I went out to spread the message of child abuse prevention, I called Daddy. I wanted to tell him about it, and explain. He didn't really understand, asking, "So, you're going to go all over Arizona and tell everyone what a bad father I was?" I explained that that wasn't it at all—that the point wasn't merely to tell stories about all the madness, but to let children who were being hurt now to know that things were going to be okay one day.

I referred back, as gently as I could, to the conversation he and I'd had when I told him I would always love him but I didn't like him very much growing up; he had not forgotten it. Now I told him how living like that throughout my childhood had felt very lonely and scary, and that I was not telling my story just to tell my story and make him seem like the "bad guy." I was telling it because I wanted children who were currently suffering to understand that they were not alone and that they would one day grow up and make a happy life for themselves.

Eventually—amazingly—Daddy genuinely seemed to understand. Every once in a while I'd have to remind him again that I wasn't speaking publicly to degrade him or to make him feel bad. I always brought it back to the children I helped. Especially when I shared stories other survivors had told me, he got it. It also helped when I told him how after one speaking engagement, a nun came up to me and said she thought it was so important and powerful that I told the crowds that I forgave Daddy for everything and that we were trying to establish a new relationship now. He liked that, and from then on, he was always okay with hearing my stories of public speaking. I even sent him all the newspaper clippings and photos from my events.

Daddy and I spoke on the phone pretty regularly during

the years he was in Florida. Sadly, I spent many of those conversations trying to talk him out of killing himself, which is why it was especially important to me that he really understand what my speaking meant—that it wasn't an attack on him, but my quest to make a difference for those suffering in the present.

Of course, his suicide talk also angered me sometimes, when I dwelled on it. But it was easier now that I lived far away, where his mood swings weren't controlling my day; it took away much of their power over me. Most of the time, I was just able to deal with each conversation with Daddy as it happened, then hang up and put it aside and move forward with my daily life.

Those were the years Daddy was trying to stop drinking. I got pockets of time when he was genuinely kind and compassionate—the man I know he was deep down, under all the vodka and beer.

His compassion about what I was trying to do in the child abuse prevention world was hugely healing for me, and for us both; it deepened my forgiveness of him enormously. It's also a big part of why I felt validated in writing this book. It was such a blessing that he understood why I do the work I do, and it was a testament to the kind of man he really was inside. I only wish he hadn't suffered so much because of his addiction and that he could have been the man he was meant to be.

— — —

I had my first speaking opportunity at a charity event within a month of being crowned. It was a domestic violence prevention event, and I was absolutely terrified beforehand. Luckily, the head of the Arizona chapter of Prevent Child Abuse America went with me to my first child abuse prevention appearance; she is an amazing person and was so kind to me. And when I was up there speaking, I cried in front of the entire little northern Arizona town that came out to see their Miss

Arizona. Everyone reacted so beautifully; I think it made me seem human and showed them they could relate to me.

After that first speech, something incredible happened: People came up to me and told me that they, too, were survivors. There was a little boy and a man who had never told anyone before. I hadn't known that would happen, and I was deeply moved by it. It was the first of so many times that people shared their lives with me after I spoke at child abuse prevention events. I feel extremely lucky that, during the course of my work, people tell me that I've helped them by sharing my story, and they now feel like they can share theirs. After that, I still got nervous before speaking events, but at least I knew that my story touched people.

Next, I spoke at an event for Mothers Against Drunk Driving, and I relished the fact that I could tell the audience that I never drank anymore and that I had never done a drug a day in my life (I can still say that!). It's especially satisfying when I speak to the junior high and high school students—and it felt particularly relevant when I was Miss Arizona USA, because I was still in college and not much older than them. I felt like I could really be an example to them of how the pattern of abusive, destructive behavior can stop—and of how they could be strong enough to stop it.

Lots of other speaking engagements followed throughout the year I was Miss Arizona. In the beginning especially, someone usually came to give me moral support—sometimes Dave and sometimes the head of the organization, who seemed to have infinite time for this work. I got lots of letters after my speaking engagements, almost all of which I still have.

I did an early appearance at Phoenix Children's Hospital; it was one of my most memorable moments as Miss Arizona and really just one of my all-time most meaningful moments in life. I was visiting with the children, and in every room I went into they were so excited to tell me when they would be going home, and their parents would tell me too; they were all eager to share that they were close to getting to go home and back to lives of normalcy. Dave was with me that day, and one little girl who had recently had brain surgery was so enamored with both of us, but especially with Dave. She kept calling us Barbie and Ken. She was the sweetest girl, full of life and love even though she was very ill.

In the last room we visited there was a tiny new family, a young mom and dad and their beautiful little baby girl, Cheyenne. You could feel the immense love these parents had for their baby, just looking at her with such love and joy. Her parents got so excited when I came in; they were really happy that Miss Arizona was there to say hi to their daughter. Because everyone had been telling me when they'd be going home, I naively asked them when Cheyenne would get to leave the hospital. And with immense bravery and love, the mother told me their baby wasn't going home, that they had just removed her breathing support and they were waiting for her to die.

I was completely unprepared for this, and I burst into tears. These two parents began comforting me in those final moments of their beautiful child's life. The father saw that I had a stack of photos (Miss Arizona is always expected to autograph photos of herself after events), and he asked if I would make one out to Cheyenne. Her mom said they would put that picture in Cheyenne's coffin; they wanted her to have that. She said they were so happy she got to have this life moment and meet a Miss Arizona before she passed on. It helped me to know what a difference one person, one moment can make—I could have been any one of a hundred pageant girls, of course, but still it felt incredible to help these courageous, heartbroken people make memories with their little girl.

It really made me realize the significance of saying and writing someone's name; it solidifies their existence, and after they've gone, it makes them seem still here with us, somehow. It was one of those moments in life when you actually realize the impact we can all have on one another's lives. Certainly that couple's love and strength affected me forever. Several years later, after Dave and I were married and I lost our first baby in my third month of pregnancy, I remembered sweet Cheyenne and that brave couple who birthed their baby, and loved and held her and then lost her. I drew strength from that memory. If they could be so brave during that incredibly painful time, I could do the same, having never even seen the baby we lost.

I loved my time as Miss Arizona. It was amazingly rewarding and gratifying. But I also found it challenging in some ways—completely worth it, for sure, but it could be pretty exhausting and draining. The media scrutiny alone was strange. It's not like they were hard on me or anything, but I remember when I realized I had very little control over how newspapers and magazines represented me. Before all my appearances, we always sent the event organizers my headshot and a biography, and they usually gave those to their local newspapers. But press would also sometimes come to the events and take their own photos of me. I remember getting photographed for the *Arizona State Press*, the state university's newspaper. I thought it was cool, except that I hated how I looked in the picture they chose. I also learned that I could be misquoted in the press, so I started watching my words carefully. It could be frustrating sometimes, but it was also such an amazing learning experience, well beyond the work I was doing with child abuse prevention.

For the first six months or so, the speaking events affected me very deeply, and it would take me a good day to shake off the feelings. Of course, these days I still feel a lot of different things when I speak about abuse, but generally now I am pretty good at moving on from those feelings and not getting too drained or overwhelmed. Every now and again, though, when something really touches a nerve, maybe an especially powerful interaction with someone who discloses their own story afterward, I still feel like that: overwhelmed that I now have a voice when my childhood can sometimes still feel so close. To this day, I remember exactly what it was like to be a girl, powerless, in my bedroom that was plastered wishfully in magazine covers and photos, and feeling so completely isolated and like no one cared about what I was going through. And now that I'm helping others in abusive situations—young girls and boys, and even grown women—I'm sometimes floored by it, still. Those speaking engagements are as healing for me as they are for those brave people I speak to.

After my time as Miss Arizona USA was over, I continued to speak out about child abuse and domestic violence. Volunteering my time for the last eighteen years has not always been easy. The challenges have changed over the years—at first, it was tricky to juggle school and work and speaking engagements; then when I had babies, it was difficult to figure out how to take care of them, be a good wife, and continue with my speaking events. I had to learn how not to give so much of myself away at those events that I was too spent to be really present for the babies. It took time to find a balance, but I gradually did.

It has also not always been easy making myself vulnerable to other people's judgment. Sometimes, arriving at a speaking engagement, I am instantly stigmatized when people learn that I am a former Miss Arizona. It's gotten better as I age; it was way worse in my twenties and even my early thirties. But I still see those looks sometimes; I know them well by now. I've gotten them from kids in junior high, and from older women on boards and committees with me—sometimes they would say I couldn't understand things because I was still too young. Now, mostly, I get more respect because I've been in the world of child abuse prevention longer. But people who don't know me sometimes still look down their noses when they find out a former Miss Arizona is involved in whatever task is at hand. I get it, but it doesn't make it any less hurtful.

Anyone who thinks I do this because I crave the limelight couldn't be more wrong. It can be draining and unsettling, at times. My life would be far more peaceful if I never did another public appearance. But I remain ready and willing to open myself up to all of it because I've had enough experiences when someone has said to me, "I was thinking about killing myself and your story made me feel better"; or, "I know how you felt because that's how I feel now—I don't want to go home to my dad." Those exchanges make it all worthwhile, because I know how much a connection like that would have meant to me when I was a scared little girl.

— — —

Soon after I gave up my Miss Arizona USA title, Daddy did as he often did and came to the rescue of his family. Grandmother Parisa had started having strokes, very common in my family, and the last one had been quite debilitating. So Daddy and my uncle Azad decided to move in with her and help take care of her and the house. They all moved into a cute little townhouse back in Springfield.

I soon realized that both men were drinking all day long and, from what I heard, Uncle Azad at least was doing some drugs too. Daddy was more of a prescription drug user by then, often mixed with alcohol of course. They'd stopped smoking so much opium, for some reason; maybe they lost their dealer. In any case, that house—deceivingly cute from the outside, like all of the others he lived in—became my daddy's final home.

— — —

Serena was having her first baby, and I flew out to see them in Tennessee immediately after his birth, while they were still in the hospital. I turned in a paper for class that morning, then headed for the airport. I'd be missing my Spanish exam the next day, but I didn't care; I was so excited to meet my nephew.

And he truly was exquisite, his little face like those drawings of a perfect baby head on a jar of baby food. Daddy had come to meet him too, and we went to the hospital together. It was one of the only times I drove in the car with Daddy as an adult, and I was struck by how weird it felt. Here we were, two adults in the car together, when I was so used to being the child in the car with my grown-up daddy. I didn't get many of those moments of being a grown-up with either of my parents, and for some reason that one stands out.

At the hospital, we got into the elevator on our way to see Serena and the baby, and there was an elderly woman in there with us. She looked fragile and overwhelmed, staring at a slip of paper in her hand. I asked her if she needed help, and with obvious relief she said she did; she wasn't sure how to find her friend who was a patient at the hospital. I helped her figure out the right floor, and when she got off the elevator, I got off too, telling Daddy I was going to help this woman find her way and that he should go up to Serena's room ahead of me. But Daddy insisted on holding the elevator door and waiting while I walked the woman over to the nurses' desk. She soon found her friend, and when I got back on the elevator, Daddy was staring at me in a way he'd never looked at me before. He said, "You really are a good person," then looked away with tears in his eyes.

That day, Daddy kept asking me if Dave was going to marry me. He wanted to know details about his family and other things, like whether he played baseball or softball (he was confused about the difference between the two; baseball and softball weren't introduced to Iran until the 1990's long after Daddy left Iran)—he was asking about stuff he'd never cared about before. But the main point on his mind was whether or not I was totally confident that Dave and I were going to get married. I told him I was pretty sure we would.

They brought the baby home the next day, and I loved being near his crib and all his yummy smelling baby things. But I was also a bit distracted by worry for Daddy; in truth, I was even more worried about him than usual. There's a photograph of him from around that time; I think my aunt took it. He's holding a little baby bunny and he looks so fragile and scared. That was sort of how he seemed all the time, by then.

During this visit with Serena and the baby, he seemed especially depressed; his eyes were full of such sadness. He also had bouts of anger, but then he would be kind and reflective and almost gentle at times. It was clear that he was drinking again. Any of you who were also raised in an abusive and/or alcoholic household will recognize this: All those years of trying to determine whether or not Daddy was drunk, and thereby determine how much danger I was in at any given moment, made me something of an expert at studying other people's patterns and habits, and reading their moods. By this point, I could tell very easily if he'd been drinking.

Daddy left early—all of a sudden he just said he had to go. I walked him outside to his car. I remember he was wearing a bulky ivory-colored sweater with jeans and, as always, his cowboy boots. Thinking about him making the long drive back from Tennessee to Virginia alone, I was feeling so sad for him, and so worried, after his extra-erratic behavior on this visit. And I felt a longing, too, as I often did when we said good-bye—a longing for more, for both of us; that he could give me more as a father, and I could give him more as a daughter. I longed for more closeness between us. I watched him drive away, waving good-bye until I could no longer see his car.

CHAPTER 9

It's strange how when someone you love dies unexpectedly, a day that starts out so normal becomes a day like no other, all its unmemorable minutia suddenly becomes magnified and significant. I'd been in a pissy mood that day, for no apparent reason. It was two days after I got back from my trip to meet my nephew; four days since I'd seen Daddy. Before heading into work at the animal clinic, I'd gone to the grocery store and picked out a bunch of Valentine's Day cards. I bought sugar cookie mix with little hearts in the dough, so when you baked them, Valentine hearts would appear in the cookies; I'd been planning to make them for Dave, but I never did.

I went back to my apartment, put the groceries away, and was walking back to my bedroom to change for work when Dave showed up unexpectedly. I was standing in the hallway. He told me that my father had died of a heart attack the night before—February 9, 1998. Everyone had been trying to get ahold of me, so he'd driven over to find me. Here is what I remember about that moment; I can see it as though I were witnessing it from the outside: I fell down onto the floor— when people say, *My legs gave out on me*, that's literal; my legs actually could not hold my body up; it must be all the extra weight from the newly heavy heart. I lay there sobbing. Dave tried to comfort me, but the poor guy hadn't had so much as a splinter his whole life, so he really didn't know how to respond to grief or what to do with this heap on the floor.

Eventually, I stood back up and got on the phone, and was

immediately plunged into the endless details that accompany the death of a family member: telling people, setting up the funeral, ordering the headstone. Over the next several days, my uncles tried to take care of most of it for us, for which I was grateful.

It was my aunts who had made the calls to close family and who'd told us it was a heart attack. But as soon as I regained my sense of reason, and especially when I talked to Serena, we agreed that it just didn't make sense. He had never had heart trouble; no one in our family had heart trouble. Every sudden death is shocking and impossible to grasp, but this cause of death seemed improbable on a more realistic level. Serena's mother-in-law called around to all the hospitals in the area to find out details, and she learned that Daddy hadn't been admitted to any of them. So I called my cousin Saeed, and he called my aunts, who told him the real story. They'd kept it from everyone at first in an effort not to upset Serena, just home from the hospital with her new baby: Daddy didn't have a heart attack at all. One night when Grandmother Parisa wasn't home, Daddy and Uncle Azad stayed up late into the night, sitting around talking and drinking. Azad went upstairs at some point, and Daddy pulled out his gun, he shot one round into the fireplace, and then he put the gun into his mouth and pulled the trigger. Undoubtedly it was no coincidence that Daddy killed himself on the anniversary of the day his own father died.

I felt so many different things when I learned he had actually killed himself, wave after wave of emotion. The first thing I felt was anger that my family hadn't been honest with us, when of course we had a right to know. The second thing was almost a strange kind of relief, because at least it made sense, whereas a heart attack was just too hard to believe. Then I felt sad that Daddy wasn't stronger than his will to take his own life. I wished he had been able to overcome his struggles.

And I was super disappointed when I heard how much he had been drinking that night. I blame so much of his misery on alcohol. I felt unbearably sad; somehow, the fact that it was suicide made me feel even more lonely. I felt like I wasn't enough for him. I felt mad that both of my parents gave up on me. In those first moments after you learn about the suicide of a loved one, you feel all of those things, and more.

I also instantly started playing back those last few days with him. All those questions he'd been asking me—it had been so unlike Daddy—started making sense. I think he was making sure I'd be okay when he left me.

— — —

Dave and I flew to Virginia the day after we found out. A couple of days after that was Dave's birthday—the day before the funeral. We tried to acknowledge it, Sue and Michelle came over and we had cupcakes. It wasn't much of a celebration, but I didn't want to completely ignore the love of my life's birthday, even though we were going to be burying Daddy within twenty-four hours.

Serena and I selected the grave marker together and decided what to put on it. People joke about that—"When I die I want it to say . . . on my headstone." But when you really get down to choosing what is going to be carved into that grave marker forever, it's really pretty unsatisfying. An entire life gets summed up on a tiny piece of stone; there's not enough room. Serena and I thought about what Daddy loved and settled on an image of a dogwood flower, because he loved to garden and we had a dogwood tree in our backyard growing up, and we also had a few jets engraved on it.

We buried Daddy on Valentine's Day. It was freezing cold. Sue drove to the cemetery with us, and she was being extra funny, trying to make Serena and me feel a little bit lighter, and we laughed a lot during that car ride. I remember feeling guilty about laughing on the way to bury Daddy, but in retrospect I see how much we needed it.

Once we stepped out of the car, though, reality hit us in the face faster than the whipping wind. Nobody smiled once, through the whole ceremony. Everyone acts so heavy when someone kills himself. There's all this pained pity for the bereaved, and awkwardness too, every time someone looks at you; this is on top of your grief and sorrow. Serena and I held on to each other, sobbing, as they put Daddy in the ground. We were in our mid-twenties and now officially on our own. Life felt terribly lonely, scary, and sad.

Compounding our grief was the bizarre fact that my aunts and uncles had decided not to tell Grandmother Parisa that her eldest child was dead. And so after watching my daddy's plain pine casket get lowered into the ground, after watching the men shovel dirt onto his casket and then lay sod over him, which just made it feel so final, we went back to my grandmother's house and pretended that he had merely taken off somewhere, that none of us knew where and we were all confused as to why he'd left but that he was definitely alive somewhere in this world. Within a day, my relatives came up with a better story: They told her he had decided to go back to Iran and had left them a letter they didn't want her to see.

Grandmother Parisa knew this was bogus—hadn't he just moved back to Virginia from Florida to take care of her after her stroke? In the days after he died, my grandmother would take my face in her hands and ask me in Farsi, "Where is he?" She knew I was a terrible liar. For that entire weekend, whenever she asked us about him, Serena and I would just cry and pretend we couldn't remember how to say it in Farsi, then leave the room. It seemed a ridiculously cruel thing to do to her. I begged them to tell her, up until her own death five years later. She just went on wondering where he was, right up to the day we buried her—next to her son, who, as far as she knew, had simply vanished off the face of the earth.

However good my family's intentions, it still seems to me—sixteen years later and with Grandmother Parisa long buried—like an awful thing to do to her, not telling her that her first-born child had blown his brains out in her basement. But I also sometimes wonder if maybe they were right; maybe they spared her the nightmares; maybe they spared her the heartache of knowing that someone who supposedly loves you has decided you really weren't worth sticking around for after all.

— — —

We went through all of Daddy's belongings in the days after the funeral. I kept a lot of stuff, and still have it, in a blue plastic bin here in my house. We also gave a lot of things away. Saeed wanted his model jet planes; I was glad of that.

I started in the bathroom and it felt so odd, cleaning out my daddy's toothbrush and shampoo. In his bedroom I found the Great Dane calendar I had given him that previous Christmas. Though he died on February 9, the calendar was still open to January. It was one of the thousands of details that broke my heart. The fact that he hadn't bothered to flip the page to the next month seemed like such a symbol of how he had already given up, even before our last weekend with him. He didn't care enough about living to keep the calendar current; the days had all run together for him. I still have that Great Dane calendar. Maybe when I kick it, someone will find it among my possessions and wonder why the heck I had it.

Among Daddy's possessions was a small, blue, tin safe with a rolling lock on the front. He'd had it our whole lives. He would hide stuff in there, and I was always so curious about what was in it. What I found in that box after he died was like finding the real substance inside my daddy—all the parts of him I think he really wished he could have been, but just couldn't.

The box contained all the cards I had sent him since he moved out—every single birthday, Christmas, holiday, and "just because" card I'd given him over the previous six years. He had also saved every last memento from my year as Miss Arizona, all the newspaper clippings, all the photos he'd taken at the pageant, and all the pictures I'd sent him. I had sent him a photo of one of my first appearances in a classroom of what looks like about fourth graders. It was one of those occasions when I got to explain to him that I wasn't traveling the state in order to bash him, but to provide a source of inspiration and hope for children. The fact that he'd kept it still means a lot to me. It makes me feel better about telling my story—his story—and it helps me to know that he understood why I have to do so.

The blue metal box held something else that's special to me: a note I wrote to Daddy when I was eight years old and had accidentally broken the sink in the guest bathroom. In our house, if you broke something, accident or not, you paid for it. I was terrified of how angry he'd be, not so much of the pushes or slaps or punches I would receive, but more of that awful look in his eyes—like you were the most loathsome human being on the planet—and then of being ignored for days. When that happened, it wasn't merely as if your presence was unwanted; it was like you truly didn't exist, there in your own home, for days and days. I still feel the effects of it to this day. Anyway, I knew I was going to get it, so I thought I'd try to head off the punishment by writing him an apology note and giving him all the money I had. For all those years, Daddy had kept my note.

He kept his wedding ring in that box from his marriage to Patty. I think he loved her until the day he died; never try to make sense of the heart.

Daddy was not one to keep everything; he kept all those things in his blue safe because they were important to him, because I was important to him. When your parent decides to leave this world forever, it's those little things you can hold on to that really help you through the dark moments.

— — —

The week I returned home to Arizona after the funeral, I went back to work at the animal clinic, and I got right back into my studies too. I was trying to keep my mind constantly busy. For that same reason, I decided to go ahead with a pageant that I had planned to enter before Daddy died. Maybe I also did it in part because that was one of the things that Daddy and I had talked about during those last few days I saw him. The pageant was a preliminary to compete in the Miss Arizona pageant for the Miss America system, the title I held earlier was the Miss Arizona USA title, for the Miss USA system. The Miss America system required a talent that is performed on stage, and I had planned to do a Persian dance. At first, Daddy was a bit concerned—he wanted to make extra sure that I never danced for money. But then he understood, once I explained that dancing at a Miss Arizona preliminary pageant was the furthest thing from that. And then he actually tried to give me guidance on it! It was very sweet; he told me about some famous belly dancers, though my dance was not really going to be very traditional. My costume looked kind of like Jasmine's outfit, from the Disney movie.

Could there have been a worse time for me to compete in a pageant? To really seal the deal, in a genius move I decided that, in light of Daddy's death, I should change my platform from child abuse prevention to suicide prevention. I cried the whole night—up on stage, while competing. Needless to say, I did not win that one. It was the first and last preliminary competition in which I was allowed, as I had aged out of the Miss America system, at twenty-four. Still, I loved my years on the pageant circuit.

More helpfully, after I got back from the funeral, I talked with a counselor at school a few times. She actually cried when I told her my story; it was touching. Of course, I probably cried too, for the duration of every visit with her. I talked to her about the nightmares I had started having shortly after Daddy died. While no one can say the magical thing that will ease your pain during a time like that, it still helped to have somewhere calm and quiet to go and talk to someone who didn't shy away from the subject of suicide, someone who would sit there with me and my grief for as long as I wanted to keep coming back.

— — —

When someone dies, you almost have to believe in angels or ghosts, an afterlife of some sort, to keep your sanity. Otherwise it is simply too devastating and final, and impossible, for a while, to accept that they are just gone—literally nowhere. Shortly after Daddy died, I started reading books about the afterlife. I was having lots of dreams about him, many in which he was stuck somewhere, trying to get out. I also thought I could feel him around me, though not as strongly as I felt Grandmother Elizabeth.

Those dreams and impressions of visitations eventually landed me among hundreds of other poor saps in a resort conference room with a gaudy chandelier and a carpet that made the chandelier look tame, at a—wait for it—spiritual medium seminar! Yes, I was on my way to the deep end, in my desperation to believe Daddy still existed somewhere.

The man who claimed to be a spiritual medium had an enormous entourage. I watched them before he started; they were scouring the audience, I'm sure for especially susceptible people to call on during the show—which is exactly what it was, a show. In spite of myself, I wanted more than anything to be called on, but his people didn't pick me; I must have looked too skeptical. If they noticed me, I'm sure they pegged me as someone who wouldn't play along, and they were probably right. But at the time, and for a few years after Daddy died, I was very nearly vulnerable enough to fall for a charade like that.

— — —

If Daddy's death was hard to accept, it was even tougher to digest the fact that he had committed suicide. I think that's true for most people—suicide is just kind of inconceivable, even, or maybe especially, when it affects your life directly. Recently, I was at a speaking event and a young girl approached me afterward and said, "My dad died too; he took a lot of pills and he died." I asked, "He took those pills on purpose?" and she nodded yes. And I said what this sweet girl couldn't actually articulate out loud: "So your daddy killed himself, like mine did." She nodded yes again. Poor girl, she couldn't even say the word suicide. And actually, even when it hasn't touched people's lives directly, I can often see them struggle with the concept, and with the word itself.

I learned, after Daddy died, that it's very common to be in denial about the suicide of a loved one. I read every book I could find on the topic. I know I was in denial about his suicide for at least a few years. It didn't help that our extended family forced us to pretend he was still alive whenever we spoke with or saw my grandmother Parisa. Serena and I would have conversations with her, in our broken Farsi and using hand gestures, about how Daddy had moved back to Iran. As a result, I really thought there was a chance it wasn't real, that maybe Daddy was actually still alive. I even remember that Serena and I came up with some scenarios for why our uncles might have said Daddy was dead: money troubles, maybe; or he might have had to disappear because someone wanted to hurt him. Given the life he'd led, and the way he usually treated people, it seemed possible.

For a while, I would "see" him everywhere—once at the gas station, another time at our local breakfast eatery. Once I was sure I saw him at a casino on a weekend trip to Las Vegas, and I followed this poor guy around the casino until he actually started heading toward security. Eventually I realized that he was not my daddy, but even then, I liked watching him because he looked so much like Daddy. That's one of the saddest parts of death—you never get to see the person's face again. You never get to watch him walk into a room; you never get to see him drink from a cup of tea or eat a meal. The knowledge that you will never, ever, see the person again is just awful and overwhelming.

Serena and I both started having nightmares—about guns, about scary zombie-like ghosts, about Daddy trying to take us with him to the "other side." Finally, Serena decided she had to know for certain, and she called the police station and asked if she could go down there and see the pictures of Daddy's body. I never saw them, and never wanted to, but Serena's description of the photographs of Daddy, dead, still plays in my mind to this day. She said the hole in his head was actually really small, which I found somewhat comforting. I had imagined that he'd lost at least half his head, partly because our uncle had told us that he and our cousin had to clean up the blood and brain matter in the basement, so that my grandmother would never know what had occurred, right there in her own home.

— — —

After Daddy died, I read and reread the letter Grandmother Elizabeth had written seven years earlier, when he had tried to kill himself and instead shot a hole through the closet wall. I found these two lines especially comforting: "Don't ever lose faith in yourself and remember that none of this is of your making. And whatever your Father is doing now or does in the future is of his own choosing." She had been gone for three years by this point, yet she was still giving me solace from above. I needed her reassurance and the memory of her love desperately during those years. Without them, I might easily have been consumed by grief and by the guilt I felt about his unhappiness.

And that is another big part of the complexity of losing a

loved one to suicide—the guilt that comes in the aftermath is so heavy and damaging. Still today, I sometimes find myself worrying that something I did or didn't do somehow contributed to him choosing to end his life, and in those moments, no psychologist or suicide expert could tell me otherwise. I understand that most people who kill themselves are suffering from some type of mental illness. But I am also fairly certain that part of Daddy's misery, late in life, had to do with our relationship—specifically, with the guilt he felt about abusing me. He must have periodically replayed the conversation in which I had told him I didn't like him. And I know it pained him that I traveled around Arizona telling people about how he beat me. It's possible, too, that he remembered the inappropriate moments with me. More than once I've wondered if all of those dark memories and feelings involving me amplified his self-loathing.

I also felt guilty about small things, like the wolf shirt he'd asked me to get for him when he visited me for the Miss Arizona pageant. It was still on my to-do list when he died. I thought about that silly shirt for years.

I've often wondered: Why didn't he wait to kill himself until he'd seen me get married? Until I was settled down? Why didn't he feel like I needed him around? And the answer I always come up with is that he saw that I was, finally, doing well and that I was going to be okay. I was a working college student, a former Miss Arizona, immersed in Dave's lovely family and on a path to marrying into it. I even wonder if seeing me help that sweet old woman in the hospital—seeing that I would be okay because I was a "good person"—was part of it. That he thought I would be okay without him at this point; Serena too, now that she had a family of her own. And then I'll wonder: If I hadn't had it all together, if I'd been more of a mess, if I had seemed helpless and lonely, would he have thought I needed him more . . . and would he therefore not have killed himself? Did he just decide, during that last visit when he met his grandson and saw his daughters thriving, that it would be all right to leave us? Whatever you might call this line of thought—an overdeveloped sense of guilt or magical thinking—I know it's not realistic. And yet I still find myself pursuing it, and I still have to step back and remind myself that he did not kill himself because of me.

Writing this book, and looking more closely at all my feelings about Daddy's suicide, this possibility occurred to me: Maybe we survivors of a loved one's suicide actually need to feel the guilt; maybe we need to feel like somehow we played a part in their choosing to leave us, because then at least we know we entered their minds. In some way, their decision to leave us hurts a little bit less if we believe it was because of us. That way, we can feel like they gave us a second thought before ending it all and abandoning us. But really, what do I know—my college degree is in English?

In any event—just in case you didn't notice the first two or three times I said it!—I want to be very clear that we must not blame ourselves when someone we love takes their own life. I'm trying to be honest here about my own experience, about the burden of guilt I carry, so that other readers who feel the same kinds of things might see that they're not alone in those painful feelings. Acknowledging and examining those feelings of guilt and responsibility is an important step in healing. But we have to be careful not to believe them. If my daddy's guilty feelings about abusing me made him hate himself more, that is not my fault, however much I have worried that it is over the years. In my rational mind, I know I am not to blame. But I can still get caught up in the guilt, and I still have to remind myself that I did not cause him to kill himself. I hope any of you who have lost someone to suicide will also remind yourselves of that, whenever the dark thoughts come.

You know what doesn't help? The way some people react

when you tell them that someone you love has committed suicide. They'll get this weird expression on their faces, a mixture of horror and something like accusation—as if you yourself did or didn't do something crucial that caused your father to take his own life. I'm sure they don't mean it, and I'm sure most people aren't even aware they're acting so awkwardly. But it almost seems like they're afraid of suicide, and of you—like being near you now, they might be tempted to kill themselves too; like I have some magic power that causes people to vanish, which, in some of my lower moments, I sometimes kind of think I do. After all, how many people are abandoned by both their parents and their stepparent? Once in a while when I'm in a certain frame of mind, I think, "Maybe it *is* me . . . maybe those people are right to look at me like that!" It's strange, the power of that kind of thinking, even after all these years, and everything I've done to try to heal myself, and the work I do to help other people. It takes vigilance not to buy into those thoughts.

I've received more condolence cards and calls when my cats and dogs have died than I did when Daddy died. Some friends never acknowledged it at all, which was so disconcerting and hurtful. It only adds to the pain and confusion that comes when someone you love commits suicide. If you take nothing else away from this book, at least take this: If you know someone whose life is affected by suicide, do me a favor and do not ignore the fact that someone they love has died. Grieve with and for them like friends do, and don't treat them like a freak because of their loved one's bad decision.

— — —

In addition to finding solace in my grandmother's letter, after Daddy died I also felt grateful to my high school counselor, for that long-ago conversation in which she'd told me I should prepare myself for the day that he would actually succeed at committing suicide. Her words, and the fact that I actually listened to her, saved me from even more pain on the day Daddy killed himself and the dark guilty days that followed.

Someone recently asked me how, exactly, I went about "preparing" for something as terrible as the possibility of my father's suicide. I said I did pretty much the same thing I do when preparing for something positive, like winning Miss Arizona: I would visualize the day Daddy succeeded in killing himself. I'd actually sit and imagine what life would be like without him, how I would feel. Then I would let myself feel that feeling and deal with it, though it wasn't yet real. I would think it through, really explore it and experience it. It sounds kind of morbid and weird now that I write it, but I just thought to myself, "Okay, worst-case scenario, Daddy does kill himself— what will life be like and how will I deal with it?" And I saw that, like with every other bad thing that had happened in my life, I would need to choose between becoming hopelessly mired in fear and sadness, or moving forward.

Something else that came out of my preparation: Whenever I spoke to him or saw him, I thought, "What if this is my last conversation with Daddy—how would I want to treat him?" I wanted to be able to live with our last conversation, whenever that might be, and so I tried to make every conversation end well.

Another thing that really helped me after his death was the fact that I had unburdened myself when I told him how I felt about all the years of abuse. I know I said earlier that that same conversation also contributes to my guilty feelings about his suicide; nothing is ever simple, is it? But it really is both things. Even though I can still feel the heavy-heartedness of that day, I know that telling him also probably saved my sanity when he died. I'm glad I shared what I did with Daddy. I'm glad I got it all out and none of it was trapped inside my mind or my heart when he shot and killed himself. There was nothing left unsaid when he died.

About guilt and regret, I have one more thing to say: Sometimes that baggage tries to creep its way into our lives, but the crucial thing to remember is that *we* get to control whether or not we're going to dwell on it—and we get to decide we don't want to. That choice is up to us, to live in the present moment with the new families we've made (whether that is friends or boyfriends or girlfriends or spouses or children or extended family) and not to waste a single moment of today's joy by focusing on yesterday's pain.

CHAPTER 10

The death of someone you love is such a surreal experience. You're instantly immersed in a grief that seems endless and boundless. It is always there—not just *with* you, but it also feels like it's *inside* you, physically; like it's *of* you. But then, despite its overwhelming presence, you have moments of being distracted by other parts of your life: a hectic day at work, a lighthearted moment with friends; and you have a little while when, mercifully, you're not completely consumed by the person's absence. And then it strikes you all over again, often at the oddest times, that the person is really gone, for real, forever, and it is just unbelievable.

Yet in the midst of—and in spite of—all that grief and reflection, life somehow does keep moving on. My life moved forward in all the small ways, for starters. You still have to go grocery shopping; you still have to pay all your bills on time.

Life moves on in big ways too. Sue got married that summer, as did two of my other dear friends. I got a grown-up job at Aetna. Two years after Daddy died, Dave and I got married; Hassan, my favorite uncle, walked me down the aisle. Dave and I had a beautiful baby girl, and a couple of years later, a beautiful baby boy, and they've grown big and amazing, with two parents who adore them beyond words and two spectacular grandparents too (my in-laws).

I continued to volunteer and work in child abuse prevention; it's been over eighteen years now. As I mentioned, I started my own nonprofit family advocacy foundation, Winged Hope, in an effort to help educate the community and prevent and treat child abuse and domestic violence. Also, just as I'd wished for as a child, I started my own beauty, style, and pop culture magazine, called *Savvy*. A couple of years back, a good friend from high school got in touch to say how great it was that I'd published a magazine, because she could remember seeing all those glossy covers plastered all over my walls and hearing me talk about how I wanted to make my own one day.

Life just keeps pushing forward. Your heart is broken, but nonetheless, good things can happen; you can feel happy again. That's part of the reason I wanted to share my story—to be an example, for anyone who is struggling through a hardship, of how things get better. If you don't give up and you hold on to hope, you can turn your life into anything you desire.

Of course, sad things happen too, like the deaths of Grandmother Parisa and Grandfather Larry. I still feel the loss of all my grandparents, acutely sometimes. But when they died, I knew I was going to be okay without them. They themselves had helped give me the strength and the capacity for love that allowed me to continue on in their absence.

One of the main reasons life got better for me was that I continued to understand and empathize with Daddy and to deepen my forgiveness, even after his death. This happened in an especially powerful way after I had my kids and saw how hard it can be to be a parent. Once I became a mama, I realized how remarkable it was that he didn't abandon my sister and me after Patty left us. Being a new parent to two babies is hard enough even when you speak the primary language of your country, have a spouse, and life is generally good. My daddy was on his own, heartbroken, in a strange place surrounded by foreign people and suffering from addiction. It must have been incredibly hard for him, and I couldn't fully understand that until I had children myself.

Part of what allowed me to forgive my daddy is knowing

that my standards for my life—my need for normal and my desire to fill every day with as much happiness as possible— were not his own standards or anywhere near to his way of living. Another part was knowing, not making excuses for him, but just knowing that chemically, factually, Daddy truly could not control his drinking even though he really did want to, many times during his life. I just felt like my daddy wasn't equipped with something essential. I'm not sure what that something is, but it's necessary to function in this world, and he didn't have it. It's almost like Daddy was too sensitive for this world, so he tried to drown that sensitivity in alcohol, and it turned to anger. And that angry man seemed better equipped to handle the world than the sensitive man beneath the alcohol. Below the alcohol and the depression was a sweet man, and I didn't get to see that person often enough.

Forgiveness is really the key: Forgiveness helps strip away the anger and fear. Forgiveness allows our hearts to expand and creates space for us to pursue all the things we want, all that happiness and love, all our dreams.

I also firmly believe my faith in God helped me keep peace in my heart throughout my life. My belief that no matter what was going on, God had a bigger plan for my life and He had a plan to use all that was bad for good. That helped me through so many painful times. It also helped me in forgiveness, because I knew He would want that.

It's been sixteen years since my daddy died. His grave marker is looking pretty banged up, so Serena and I are going to order him a new one. There aren't many gestures you can perform for a loved one after they die, but that's one we decided we want to do.

※ ※ ※

People sometimes ask me what I have told my children, who are not yet teenagers, about my childhood and how I decide when to tell them certain parts, if at all. They know bits and pieces; I tell them things when I think they're relevant. They know my daddy used to hit me sometimes and that he was an alcoholic. They know that's why I do my work in child abuse prevention and why I'm writing this book that they can't read.

I only very recently told them how my daddy died. I decided to do it while they're still young, yet not so young they can't grasp the concept. Suicide is getting talked about more and more in their school, and I didn't want them to think I was keeping it a secret because it's got a stigma. I did worry a little bit about telling them because I've read that, upon learning that a loved one has committed suicide, some children may think that is their legacy and it can give them the idea to do it themselves.

Before I told them, I made a list of all the things that are important for any child to know about suicide: that it was no one's fault that Daddy killed himself and that no one could have prevented it. I told them they would never need to feel that desperate and helpless, because they are surrounded by parents and extended family and friends who love them. I reminded them, as I do every night before bed, that I will love them always and forever no matter what. I said that whatever problem they might have, it is never so big that suicide is the answer. I explained that now they can be sensitive to how often people jokingly say they are going to "kill themselves" and that they should not to be so flip about something so serious.

As always, God's timing was perfect, because within weeks of that conversation with my babies, five people in our broader circle committed suicide—friends of friends and the parents of some classmates. I shared that list I'd made with two of the families who lost someone, to help them talk about it with their children. And for all five families, reeling from suicide, I bought a book that helped me in my grieving. I was also able to have honest, important conversations with my children about these tragedies. I'm relieved to have lifted the stigma of suicide in my home.

As for what I haven't told them yet—kids are smart; they know when you're not telling them something, so I'm just really open about it—I say that I don't tell them certain things because they're unpleasant and I don't want them to think about these things if they don't have to. And then I read them both a passage from one of my favorite books, *The Hiding Place* by Corrie Ten Boom:

Once—I must have been ten or eleven—I asked Father about a poem we had read at school the winter before. One line had described "a young man whose face was not shadowed by sexsin." I had been far too shy to ask the teacher what it meant, and Mama had blushed scarlet when I consulted her.

"Sex," I was pretty sure, meant whether you were a boy or a girl, and "sin" made Tante Jans very angry, but what the two together meant I could not imagine. And so, seated next to Father in the train compartment, I suddenly asked, "Father, what is sexsin?"

He turned to look at me, as he always did when answering a question, but to my surprise he said nothing. At last he stood up, lifted his traveling case from the rack over our heads, and set it on the floor.

"Will you carry it off the train, Corrie?" he said. I stood up and tugged at it. It was crammed with the watches and spare parts he had purchased that morning.

"It's too heavy," I said.

"Yes," he said, "And it would be a pretty poor father who would ask his little girl to carry such a load. It's the same way, Corrie, with knowledge. Some knowledge is too heavy for children. When you are older and stronger you can bear it. For now you must trust me to carry it for you."

Then I tell my monkeys, "Some of Mama's past is just too heavy for you to carry right now."

So after all of this, who am I? I'm every single experience that I've had over these last forty years: I'm the scared girl who thought about killing her own father. I'm the brave girl who got on a stage and told the world her story of surviving abuse. I'm the lonely girl abandoned by both of her parents. I'm the empowered girl who knows that God is always on her side. I'm the shamed girl in the shower who doesn't understand the sickness this world holds. I'm the strong woman who is the mama of two amazing babies. I'm every one of those people, at all times. Fortunately the strong, brave woman usually wins out. And isn't that what we all are—a compilation of all of our life experiences, of little pieces of all the people who have shaped our days; all of us just fighting to make sure the best parts of us win out every day? My hope is that by sharing my story, it will help you feel brave enough to share the parts of your story that maybe no one has ever heard. That you can begin to heal and discover who you are, despite, and because of, all of your own life experiences.

Resources

Below are some resources I found helpful and thought you might, too. Please remember that no book or website can replace the help of a qualified doctor/therapist. You can also find many valuable resources on www.wingedhope.com

The Adverse Childhood Experience Test
Reprinted with permission from Vincent J. Felitti, MD

What's My ACE Score?

Prior to your 18th birthday:

1. Did a parent or other adult in the household often or very often...
    - Swear at you, insult you, put you down, or humiliate you? or
    - Act in a way that made you afraid that you might be physically hurt?   If yes, enter 1 _____

2. Did a parent or other adult in the household often or very often...
    - Push, grab, slap, or throw something at you? or
    - Ever hit you so hard that you had marks or were injured?   If yes, enter 1 _____

3. Did an adult or person at least 5 years older than you ever...
    - Touch or fondle you or have you touch their body in a sexual way? or
    - Attempt or actually have oral, anal, or vaginal intercourse with you?   If yes, enter 1 _____

4. Did you often or very often feel that ...
    - No one in your family loved you or thought you were important or special? or
    - Your family didn't look out for each other, feel close to each other, or support each other?
                    If yes, enter 1 _____

5. Did you often or very often feel that ...
   - You didn't have enough to eat, had to wear dirty clothes, and had no one to protect you? or
   - Your parents were too drunk or high to take care of you or take you to the doctor if you needed it?

   If yes, enter 1 _____

6. Was a biological parent ever lost to you through divorce, abandonment, or other reason?   If yes, enter 1 _____

7. Was your mother or stepmother:
   - Often or very often pushed, grabbed, slapped, or had something thrown at her? or
   - Sometimes, often, or very often kicked, bitten, hit with a fist, or hit with something hard? or
   - Ever repeatedly hit over at least a few minutes or threatened with a gun or knife?

   If yes, enter 1 _____

8. Did you live with anyone who was a problem drinker or alcoholic, or who used street drugs?

   If yes, enter 1 _____

9. Was a household member depressed or mentally ill, or did a household member attempt suicide?

   If yes, enter 1 _____

10. Did a household member go to prison?

   If yes, enter 1 _____

Now add up your "Yes" answers: _____
This is your ACE Score

Add up the points for a Score of 0 to 10. The higher the score, the greater the exposure, and therefore the greater the risk of negative consequences. Read more at www.acestudy.org.

5 Ways You Can Prevent Child Abuse

Reprinted with permission from Winged Hope Family
Advocacy Foundation

1. Be a nurturing, loving, patient parent. Tell your children often that they are loved and valued. Never use violence.

2. Reach out to neighbors and friends with children. Sometimes parents just need a sympathetic ear to help them feel they are not alone.

3. Be patient with crying infants. NEVER shake a baby. Step away and practice relaxation techniques before you pick up your crying infant again if you feel yourself getting stressed out.

4. Educate yourself and your community about child abuse. Arrange for a child abuse prevention speaker to attend your next HOA or PTA meeting.

5. Report suspected abuse at 1-800-4-A-CHILD

A Domestic Violence Safety Plan

Reprinted with permission from Winged Hope Family
Advocacy Foundation

- Keep a copy of important documents/papers at a trusted friend or outside family member's home.

- Be sure you have gas in your car at all times.

- Be sure you have a phone with you at all times.

- Try to set aside money and keep at a trusted friend's home.

- Keep a written list of important phone numbers with you.

10 Signs You Might Be in an Abusive Relationship
Reprinted with permission from Winged Hope Family
Advocacy Foundation

Does your partner....

1. Act jealous or possessive?
2. Make threats to hurt you or those you love, including pets?
3. Threaten to hurt him or herself if you end the relationship?
4. Pressure you sexually?
5. Cause you to feel afraid all or most of the time?
6. Try to make you feel worthless?
7. Withhold approval or affection as a form of punishment?
8. Physically or emotionally abuse you?
9. Control your access to money?
10. Isolate you?

Important Phone Numbers

Teen Lifeline
  1-800-248-TEEN

National Suicide Prevention Hotline
  1-800-TALK (8255)

Child Abuse Prevention Hotline
  1-800-4-A-CHILD

The National Domestic Violence Hotline
  1-800-799-7233

Helpful Book

No Time to Say Goodbye: Surviving the Suicide of a Loved One
  By Carla Fine

Book Club Questions

1. Discuss ways Jessica's life might have turned out differently if her mother had never left the family.

2. Throughout the book there are some instances of missed opportunities when someone could have intervened and reported the child abuse that was going on in the Shahriari home. If you were one of those who knew of the abuse, what would you have done?

3. In what ways do you think being raised in an Iranian home shaped Jessica's upbringing?

4. How different do you think the message of this book would be if Jessica didn't have her friends?

5. Throughout the book, Jessica describes her feelings and reactions to her father's unpredictability. How do you think you would have responded to his behaviors?

6. Jessica describes more than one occasion of "visualizing" her future. Do you believe this works, and have you tried this in your own life?

7. The book references Jessica's constant quest for normalcy. What does a "normal" family look like to you?

8. List the people and events that contributed to Jessica's resilience and how and why they helped.

Acknowledgments

This book would literally not have been possible without Megan Hunter. Thank you for believing the world needed to know my story, and thank you for being so much more than a publisher, thank you for being a true friend.

Thank you, Wylie O'Sullivan, my new friend, for trusting me and for helping me tell my story so beautifully. Thank you for being so patient and giving every step of the way! Your constant encouragement that writing this book was the right thing to do kept me going in the hardest of moments. I will always be thankful for your empathetic guidance. And a big thanks for Catherine Broberg for her amazing attention to detail.

Thank you to all of my incredible friends, who have been the family of my heart for so many years.

Thank you to my sister, for being my "mini-Mama" for as long as I can remember.

Thank you to my Persian family for your love.

Thank you to my "bonus" sister and brother. Even though we missed out on the traditional sibling relationship, the love I feel for you both can't be compared.

Thank you to the Nicely family for welcoming me into your family 20 years ago, and every day since.

Most especially, thank you to my husband, for all of your support and thank you to my two amazing "monkeys" who show me every day that true love does exist.

About the Author

CHAD KOERBER

Jessica Shahriari Nicely is a dedicated advocate for child abuse prevention, awareness and treatment an endeavor spanning over 17 years. She is founder and CEO of Winged Hope Family Advocacy Foundation, a non-profit organization dedicated to child abuse and domestic violence prevention, awareness and treatment. Jessica is also personally dedicated to the creation and sustainability of Family Advocacy Centers, which are designed to increase the efficacy of abuse and violence investigations while reducing stress and trauma to victims.

Jessica received a B.A. Degree in English from Arizona State University and was the co-founder and co-editor of Savvy Magazine, an international beauty, style and pop culture periodical.

Jessica lives in Arizona with her husband and two children. Her websites are: www.jessicanicely.com and www.wingedhope.com